Charles Ott · Daphne du Maurier · Robley Wilson, Jr
Anonymous · William Saroyan · Sarah Orne Jewett

# Nature Fierce and Fragile

Stories of Ecology

Model Interpretations

by Johannes Greiner, Otto Möllinger
and John O'Donovan

Ernst Klett Schulbuchverlag
Stuttgart  Düsseldorf  Berlin  Leipzig

Lehrerbuch von Johannes Greiner, Freiburg; Otto Möllinger, Freiburg; John O'Donovan, Tuy l'Eveque.

**Acknowledgements**

"People's Park", originally published in *Mankind Magazine*. Copyright © Mankind Publishing Co. Reprinted by permission of Mankind Publishing Co.

"The Birds" is reprinted by permission of Curtis Brown Group Ltd, London. Copyright © the Estate of Daphne du Maurier 1952.

"A Stay at the Ocean" is reprinted by permission of Robley Wilson, Jr and A M Heath & Company Limited, London.

"Jambawal the Thunder Man", originally published in *Identity* in October 1975. Every effort has been made to trace the copyright owners of this story, but our repeated enquiries have remained unanswered. The publishers would be glad to hear from the copyright owners of this material.

"The Hummingbird that Lived through Winter" from *My Kind of Crazy, Wonderful People: Seventeen Stories and a Play*, copyright 1944 and renewed 1972 by William Saroyan, reprinted by permission of Harcourt Brace & Company.

1. Auflage    1 5 4 3 2 1 | 1998 97 96 95 94

Die letzte Zahl bezeichnet das Jahr dieses Druckes. Alle Drucke dieser Auflage können im Unterricht nebeneinander benutzt werden.

© Ernst Klett Schulbuchverlag GmbH, Stuttgart 1994. Alle Rechte vorbehalten.

Redaktion: Glenine Hamlyn, M.A.

Umschlagfoto: Bavaria, Gauting
Druck: W. Röck, Weinsberg. Printed in Germany
ISBN 3-12-577710-0

# Contents

Introduction to the Stories ................................................................. 5
Introduction to the Model Interpretations ........................................ 6

*Charles Ott*   People's Park ............................................................ 7
Summary and Teaching Notes ........................................................ 13
Summary ......................................................................................... 13
Teaching Notes ............................................................................... 14
1. Structure ..................................................................................... 14
2. Characters ................................................................................... 17
3. For further discussion ................................................................ 18
4. Presentations .............................................................................. 18

*Daphne du Maurier*   The Birds .................................................... 19
Biographical Notes ......................................................................... 44
Summary and Teaching Notes ........................................................ 45
Summary ......................................................................................... 45
Teaching Notes ............................................................................... 47
1. Structure ..................................................................................... 47
2. For further discussion ................................................................ 54

*Robley Wilson, Jr*   A Stay at the Ocean ....................................... 57
Biographical Notes ......................................................................... 72
Summary and Teaching Notes ........................................................ 73
Summary ......................................................................................... 73
Teaching Notes ............................................................................... 74
1. The story in its parts .................................................................. 74
2. Characters ................................................................................... 78
3. Dialogues .................................................................................... 79
4. For further discussion ................................................................ 80

*Anonymous*   Jambawal the Thunder Man .................................. 81
Notes ............................................................................................... 87
Summary and Teaching Notes ........................................................ 88
Summary ......................................................................................... 88
Teaching Notes ............................................................................... 90

1. Structure .................................................................. 90
2. Style ....................................................................... 95
3. For further discussion .............................................. 95
4. For further study .................................................... 95

*William Saroyan* The Hummingbird that Lived Through Winter .... 96
Biographical Notes ...................................................... 100
Summary and Teaching Notes ...................................... 101
Summary ..................................................................... 101
Teaching Notes ............................................................ 102
1. Structure .................................................................. 102
2. For further discussion .............................................. 104

*Sarah Orne Jewett* A White Heron ............................. 105
Biographical Notes ...................................................... 116
Summary and Teaching Notes ...................................... 117
Summary ..................................................................... 117
Teaching Notes ............................................................ 119
1. Structure .................................................................. 119
2. For further discussion .............................................. 126

Glossary of Literary Terms .......................................... 127

> The cassette accompanying this book contains the stories by Charles Ott, William Saroyan and Robley Wilson, Jr (Klettnummer 57772).

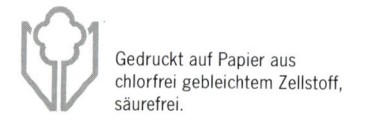

Gedruckt auf Papier aus
chlorfrei gebleichtem Zellstoff,
säurefrei.

# Introduction

"Ecology" is not a word we usually associate with fiction—so what are "stories of ecology"?

The writings in this collection all deal in various ways with the relationship between human beings and their natural surroundings. Three of the stories—one from England, one from America, one from Australia—are set at the sea: Daphne Du Maurier's "The Birds", Robley Wilson, Jr's "A Stay at the Ocean", and "Jambawal the Thunder Man", by an anonymous Aboriginal writer. In each of these, nature outwits self-satisfied human beings by departing from the familiar patterns of tides, the weather, and animal behaviour. Nature seeks revenge for the treatment humankind has given it. In "Jambawal", Aboriginal people are seen as belonging to nature, so that unjust dealings with them provoke the same reaction from the spirits as the destruction of the land.

That is the fierce side of nature. In "The Hummingbird that Lived through Winter" (William Saroyan), "A White Heron" (Sarah Orne Jewett) and "People's Park" (Charles Ott), nature is vulnerable, open to threat. A touching story involving an old, blind man and his young neighbour, "The Hummingbird" relates how a bird is lovingly restored to strength in human hands. Written a century apart, "A White Heron" and "People's Park" both have to do with choices: both raise the question of how the natural world can be appreciated by human beings without being destroyed by them.

All of these stories make good reading, and there is no lack of suspense. The reader can identify with the various characters and situations, so that the issues raised in the stories can be discussed at a personal level.

# Introduction to the Model Interpretations

The aim of these interpretations is to combine consistency of method with a concern for each story's unique character.

A short summary of the story is followed in each case by an overview, in which particular attention is paid to structure. In this way, the development of the story is illustrated. Students see how structural features such as an introductory passage, rising and falling action, a climax and an epilogue influence other elements such as suspense, atmosphere and the revelation of character.

Once students have gained general insights into the story, they are encouraged to discover the craft of the writer in more detail. Devices such as imagery, symbolism, the use of humour and the appeal to the senses are examined. Students look at the characters not only as individuals but in their relationships to each other. Focussing on the narrator, students learn to recognize the point of view used in a story and how it colours the content. Controversial issues contained in the stories are highlighted in such a way that students have to form and express their own opinions, thus learning to recognize and formulate arguments for and against a topic.

The stories themselves deal with ethical issues. Students may encounter some of these in other school subjects and will no doubt be faced with all of them in everyday life. An interdisciplinary approach is thus encouraged.

Activities for further discussion, further study and presentations take the issues beyond the stories, encouraging students to respond in an independent way, as suits their own preferences and experience.

The aim of these model interpretations is to help students to see the study of literature—in any language—as a process of discovery. It is hoped that it will be far more than an academic exercise, directly touching their own lives while increasing their understanding of the language itself.

## Charles Ott

# People's Park

The hills were a glory. I shucked off my pack and lay down my rifle just to watch the evening dusk rise like tidewater through the golden forest. The autumn sky was steel blue, the trees like a hearth fire. It was the best time of the day, the best time of year ... I found I had been holding my breath.

A wood thrush sailed over my head and landed on a sapling across the stream I had been following. It did a little bouncing dance for me, singing against the water noise, and flew away when I laughed. I decided to make camp where I was; I had covered enough territory that day. I sat on a rock beetling over a deep, clear pool and pulled out the blue plastic notebook the Park Commission insisted I keep. It wasn't much more than makework, a record of areas inspected during the day. But I knew they would cheerfully fire me, in spite of all the money I had paid them to get this job, if I was slack in anything. There were ten dozen applicants for every place in the clearing program, but I intended to stay for the full six weeks by being careful. It meant a lot to me.

It was amber dusk and then blue evening before I had my tent set up and a fire laid. I was grilling a fresh caught trout for supper when the floater arrived.

It drifted in over the stream clearing, the little wake causing a flurry of sparks from the fire. It was a basketball-sized thing on its propeller platform, all lenses and antennas. The lenses shifted as it settled to the ground.

"Hullo, Peterson," it said. I knew by the voice it was Almack, the night-duty officer back at Park Headquarters. "Is that trout you're having? It looks good, I must say."

---

1.**to shuck off** *(AE)* to remove as if peeling s.th. off – 2 **dusk** the time just before dark – 3 **hearth** [hɑːθ] fireplace – 6 **thrush** *Drossel* – **sapling** young tree – 10 **to beetle** *(AE)* to lean out – 12 **makework** work done just to keep busy – 14 **slack** careless – 18 **amber** orange or yellowish-brown – 19 **trout** [traʊt] *Forelle* – 20 **floater** *here:* small flying machine – 21 **to drift** to move slowly – **clearing** area of land without trees – **wake** *here:* wind caused by the floater – **flurry** quick movement in all directions – 23 **lens** [-z] curved piece of glass, e.g. in a camera – **to shift** to move

## 6 Charles Ott, People's Park

I was going to make some flip remark about the soy cutlet I knew Almack would have dined on, but I decided it would be cruel. "It is," I said simply. "What brings you out here at this hour?"

"You're not going to like this," he sighed, "but we want you to check up on a trace the trail sensors have reported."

"At night? I could get killed stumbling around in the dark. Let it go until morning, why don't you?"

"The trace is moving your way," he said patiently. "The infra-red picked it up and it's about the right size to be a hider. If so, he'll have to pass through here, because this is the only good pass through the hills in the area."

"He?" I snorted. "More likely, it's a brown bear with insomnia." But I added quickly, "I'll get set up." I certainly wasn't going to jeopardize my six weeks over one night's lost sleep.

"Good," said Almack. "I've got some other business to attend to, but he should arrive here in about an hour, and I'll try to return before then. Leave the radio beacon on." The floater took off quietly, rising lightly over the trees and pirouetting slowly while Almack located the moon just appearing in the east to get his bearings. Then it was gone.

I quickly doused the fire and threw the remains into the stream to kill the odor of burning wood. The tent folded easily and I brushed the ground with a bough to remove my tracks. In twenty minutes I was hidden in an outcropping of glacial rock looking down on the clearing and affording a good field of fire over the pass. After checking the clip of tranquilizer darts in my rifle, I set up the starlight scope and carefully considered every possible angle of approach. If it was a hider, he had probably left his hiding place to try to get to town, possibly for medical supplies or ammunition. If so, that made him a very stupid outlaw.

Almack returned some time later. Without the fire to guide him, the poor night vision of the floater obliged him to come in slowly, with much hesitation. Finally the floater settled near me and the fan rolled to a stop. The living silence of the forest returned. We waited.

---

1 **flip** *(AE) here:* not serious – **soy** = soya – 5 **trace** *Spur* – 12 **to snort** *schnauben* – **insomnia** inability to sleep – 13 **to jeopardize** ['dʒepədaɪz] to endanger – 17 **beacon** signal – 19 **bearings** sense of direction – 20 **to douse** [daʊs] to put out – 21 **odor** smell – 22 **bough** [baʊ] branch – 23 **outcropping of rock** *Felsenvorsprung* – 24 **to afford** to provide – **fire** *here:* shooting – 25 **clip** *Ladestreifen* – **tranquilizer** drug that makes people sleepy – **scope** *here:* telescope – 31 **to oblige** *here:* to force – 32 **hesitation** *here:* uncertain movement – **fan** propeller

## Charles Ott, People's Park

There was a small sound. I saw the hider in the spectral glow of the starlight scope, a graying middle-aged man, bent low and sniffing the air like an uncertain wolf. He traveled quickly but lightly, and he stepped into the clearing suddenly. I had no thought of "fair warning,"
no halt-you-are-trespassing-in-a-public-park. I took quick aim at his torso and fired.

There was a splash of white liquid from his belt buckle as he whirled and leapt away without a sound. "That was a bit clumsy of you," said Almack, complacent and malicious. I was up with a curse, running with high dodging steps after him. His white head appeared momentarily between two trees and I loosed a shot without pausing. It went wide.

He vanished down a ravine and I knew I had lost him. I stood panting in the clearing until Almack's floater caught up with me. "Did you notice," he asked conversationally, "whether any of the liquid had splashed on his skin?" I told him it had. "Good," he said. "It's a contact-type drug. Even a small amount should begin to slow him up shortly, I should think."

It was an order. "All right," I answered, controlling my breathing, "I'll go find him." As I entered the dimly lit forest the floater rose and went into one of the automatic holding patterns. Probably Almack had gone out for coffee.

I set out for the point where I had last seen my quarry, straining for vision in the occasional scraps of moonlight. It was a thickly grown, steeply eroded little cut he had found. I decided against entering it and walked along the edge, peering into the viscous darkness below. Presently I sat down and pulled the starlight scope from its leg holster. I was sweeping with it when he jumped me from behind.

His hands were on my neck and his knees on my back and still he made no sound. I bucked and rolled desperately, trying to hit him with the scope. His face was demonic, lit in pale planes. He shifted weight

---

1 **spectral** ghostly – **glow** steady light – 5 **to trespass** to enter without permission – 7 **liquid** ['--] *Flüssigkeit* – **buckle** *Schnalle* – **to whirl** to rotate very fast – 8 **to leap (leapt** [lept], **leapt)** to jump – **clumsy** careless, uncoordinated – 9 **complacent** [kəm'pleɪsnt] pleased with oneself – **malicious** [mə'lɪʃəs] intending to hurt – 10 **to dodge** to move rapidly to remain unseen – 13 **to vanish** to disappear – **ravine** [rə'viːn] deep, narrow valley – **to pant** to breathe quickly – 20 **dimly** poorly – 21 **pattern** *here:* position – 23 **quarry** ['kwɒrɪ] creature being hunted – **to strain** to make a great effort – 26 **to peer** to look very hard – **viscous** ['vɪskəs] thick like oil – 27 **holster** special pocket for a weapon – 28 **to sweep** *here:* to move s.th. smoothly and widely – 30 **to buck** to jump wildly – 31 **plane** flat surface

## 8 Charles Ott, People's Park

just as I heaved and momentum carried us both over the edge of the ravine, sliding and tumbling in the raw yellow soil. We rolled and clutched at each other, scrabbling through falling sheets of rocks and grit, legs flapping. I came up against a branched stump with a painful
5 jar and he careened into me and past, wrenching my leg. I heard him hit something solid, followed by a liquid splash. I blacked out.

Almack awoke me sometime later, the floater humming in front of me. "Are you all right?" he asked. "Where's the hider?"

"Down there," I grunted, motioning fuzzily, "I don't think I can
10 move."

"Well, don't worry. We'll have a police ambulance copter in here shortly to pick you up. Just relax." The floater rose out of my vision, and I lost consciousness again.

When I awoke a second time it was to sounds of pain. The hider had
15 dragged himself away from the stream, but he groaned with every move. Blood was glistening blackly on his pants as he came into my vision. I supposed he had broken some bones just as I had. "Take it easy, friend," I called. "There'll be an ambulance here shortly."

He cursed in a low voice, but gave up his efforts and settled back,
20 looking at me sourly. His labored breathing slowed. After a while he hitched himself up to a sitting position and said, "I'll bet you're real proud of yourself, capturing a genuine desperado and getting injured in the line of duty and all. You can show off your medal to the kids back at home, right? You're a hero."

25 I shouldn't have been, but I was hurt. "Look, we don't hate you," I said. "My rifle's got nothing but tranquilizer darts in it. We just need to get you out of the park. It's closed right now."

He shook his head sadly. "You're as mealy-mouthed as the bureaucrats in Washington. The park isn't closed 'right now.' It's closed for-
30 ever. You're not going to let anybody in here ever again. Then you wonder why some of us try to stay on here."

"Stop trying to act like a martyr. There'll be floater stations available to everybody for free."

---

1 **to heave** to move s.th. heavy – **momentum** force of movement – 2 **to slide** to slip, to glide along a surface – **to tumble** to fall with a rolling movement – 3 **to clutch** to hold s.th. tightly – 4 **grit** very small pieces of stone – **stump** base of a tree that has been felled – 5 **jar** *here:* a very hard hit – **to careen** to move sideways fast – **to wrench** to twist violently – 9 **to grunt** to make a low, rough sound like that of a pig – **to motion** to show by a gesture – **fuzzily** vaguely, not clearly – 15 **to groan** to make a sound of pain – 28 **mealy-mouthed** making vague, unclear statements

## Charles Ott, People's Park 9

"My God!" he cried. "Do you listen to yourself, ever? Floaters? Sitting in front of a TV screen, seeing what the machine sees, hearing the forest through a pair of earphones? You gadget-happy bastard, is that what the wilderness means to you?"

He continued into a long speech beginning with "Have you ever walked down a country road just to...," but abruptly I couldn't listen. A sick realization had come to me: I would never walk in the woods again. The Park Commission wouldn't wait for me to heal. They would just hire the next man on the list to hunt down hiders, and by the time I got out of the hospital, this and every other national park in the country would be closed. I began to weep a little.

"Shut up!" I yelled suddenly, cutting off his sappy rhapsody. "You caused this; you brought this down on us!" I was shaking and gasping, angry at the world and angry at myself for loosing it at him. "You and your nature-lovers, and conservationists, and ecology freaks. You prattled for years about getting people back to the wilderness, and they *came,* my God, how they came. Backpacks and camper busses and tents and trailers and motorbikes. It's not enough for you to admire Mother Nature; you've got to be nature-lovers and sleep with her and live with her and piss in the streams. And when we finally close off the parks so that our kids will know at least what the wilderness is, you try to hide in here and spoil even that." I stopped, and I was ashamed.

"You're grandstanding," he commented, accurately. "You know you could just have restricted the park to hiking or something. Do you really think our children are going to be uplifted by pictures of beauty they can never share?"

I was long in answering. "You know better than that. There's three hundred million people in this country. If we let everyone into the park who wanted to come, even if they just walked around and didn't drop a single beer can, it wouldn't be wild anymore. It would just be a picnic grounds. The floaters are better—they're small, and quiet, and they don't even touch the ground. People will be able to see and hear the forest forever, even if they can't touch it, because the wilderness can survive the floaters. But the people would be the death of it."

We both were silent for a long time, nursing our pain and listening to the quiet spilling of the water in the bottom of the ravine. I thought

---

3 **gadget-happy** enthused by mechanical objects – **bastard** *(slang)* very unpleasant person – 12 **sappy** full of strength and confidence – 16 **to prattle** to talk a lot about nothing – 24 **to grandstand** *(AE)* to act showily – 25 **to restrict** to limit

of what a friend this man would have made, if I'd met him somewhere else. We were two alike, and I wanted to ask his name. But he spoke first: "The woods are beautiful tonight, aren't they?" he asked, a little indistinct with the drug.

They were. The moon was high now, and in its light the trees looked touched with old pewter. There was a breeze, gentle with the scent of pine and rich moss, tasting like mineral water. "It's a shame," he said, "that the kids growing up now won't be able to smell this."

In the distance, I heard the beat of the helicopters approaching. "They're developing an olfactory unit for the floaters," I said.

---

4 **indistinct** [ɪndɪˈstɪŋt] unclear – 6 **pewter** *Zinn* – 10 **olfactory** concerned with the sense of smell

# Summary and Teaching Notes

## Summary

One autumn the narrator is spending an enjoyable vacation as a voluntary warden in a national park. While settling down for the night he receives instructions, via a mobile, remote-control device called a floater, to capture a man who is illegally hiding in the park: a "hider". When the two men eventually meet, a fierce fight ensues, and both are severely injured.

While waiting to be rescued the two men engage in a heated argument. The warden bitterly reproaches the hider and other "ecology freaks" like him for causing damage, thus forcing the authorities to close all parks. The "hider" criticizes the authorities for imposing restrictions that prevent people from enjoying nature. The reader learns of plans to close the parks completely, so that only with the aid of a television screen and a floater will nature-lovers be able to see, hear and smell the wilderness. It turns out that although the hider and the warden differ on how to protect national parks, they share a love of nature.

# Teaching Notes

## 1. Structure

Students could be asked to outline the main segments of the story first. The following division is a suggestion but by no means the only possible outline:

*Part I*
a) The setting (**5** 1–20 "arrived"): time of the year, place, time of day; background on narrator's job
b) (**5** 21–**6** 19 "it was gone"): Almack and his instructions
c) (**6** 20–**7** 22): The wait (narrator alone) and the chase (Almack watching)

*Part II*
a) (**7** 23–**8** 13): The physical struggle between the narrator and the hider
b) (**8** 14–end): the discussion between the narrator and the hider

**Part I a) The setting** (**5** 1–20)

*1. Describe the mood of the opening paragraphs.*
The story begins on a joyful note. The narrator's celebration of nature is described in emotional terms: "a glory" (**5** 1), "the best..." (**5** 4), "holding my breath" (**5** 5).

*2. Which of our senses are appealed to? Give examples.*
– Sight: e.g. "the golden forest", "...steel blue", "...like a hearth fire", "...amber dusk and then blue evening". Note the use of colour.
– Hearing: e.g. "singing against the water noise", "I laughed" (**5** 8).
– Smell and taste, e.g. "grilling a fresh caught trout for supper" (**5** 19).

*3. What information does the narrator give about himself and his job?*

He is employed by the Park Commission as part of a "clearing program" for six weeks. The job is very important to him, and he was lucky to get it. He carries a rifle and has to cover a certain amount of ground daily.

*4. Comment on the point of view of the account.*
We see everything through the eyes of the first-person narrator. This makes the account personal ("It meant a lot to me", **5** 16–17). The feelings expressed—here, of joy—seem credible, involving the reader more directly.


## Part I b) Almack and his instructions (**5** 21–**6** 19)

The "floater" arrives on the scene. The students should discuss the use and credibility of this gadget, as well as the author's purpose in inventing this futuristic type of machine.

*1. What feelings does the floater provoke?*
This way of observing people, or spying, makes one feel uneasy.

*2. Describe your first impressions of Almack from this encounter.*
He seems amiable; he is Petersen's (the narrator's) boss. One might argue that the narrator's reactions to Almack (resistance to instructions) colour our view of Almack at this point.


## Part I c) The wait and the chase (**6** 20–**7** 22)

*1. What precautions does the narrator take?*
He removes all signs of his camp, checks his rifle (it is only here that we learn it is used purely to tranquilize the hiders), covers his tracks and hides where he has a good view. Note how all this detail adds suspense.

*2. How does the narrator feel about the instructions received?*
He is very reluctant to track the hider at night but does not want to jeopardize his job by refusing.

*3. How does Almack react to the succession of events?*
He is "complacent and malicious" (**7** 9).

*4. Describe the hider.*
He is "a graying middle-aged man". This description conveys a feeling of normality, harmlessness. The hider is then compared to a wolf, a creature of nature, indicating that he lives close to nature. At the same time, however, a wolf can be a creature of threat and stealth.

**Part II a) The struggle (7 23–8 13)**

*1. Find words and phrases that make this scene dramatic.*
"…straining for vision", "peering into the viscous darkness": the narrator's vulnerability is emphasized.

The sequence of events is reminiscent of adventure stories and Westerns: a sudden, unexpected threat ("He jumped me from behind") followed by wild action. Emotional language adds suspense ("desperately", "demonic"). In contrast to Westerns, however, this fight is not between "good guys" and "bad guys" or "good" and "evil". The ensuing discussion between the hider and the narrator shows the reader that these two characters have a lot in common.

*2. How does Almack's arrival contrast with the scene that precedes it?*
Almack's lack of emotion and relaxed approach contrast sharply with the tension of the fight.

**Part II b) The discussion (8 14–end)**

The arguments can be divided into three categories:

- logical: factual proofs, cause and effect
- moral: what ought to be done, given certain circumstances
- emotional: appeal to sentiments and emotions as a final means of persuasion

Students are asked to decide which of the arguments produced by the two men fit into each category and whether they are adequate, persuasive, convincing, or otherwise.

1. *The following outline can be elaborated on the blackboard:*

| The hider | The warden |
|---|---|
| Emotional, sarcastic criticism (**8** 21–24). | Calm, reassuring tone, gives reasons for his actions, a logical argument (**8** 25–27). |
| First reacts vehemently, rudely, then presents a logical argument tinged with self-pity (**8** 28–31). | He chides the hider, trying to refute his argument (**8** 32–33). |
| Another emotional attack on the warden's insensitivity leading into reminiscences on his first-hand experience of nature (**9** 1–6). | A pause: The warden does not listen any more. *Why not?* Then follows an emotional, moralizing counter-attack combined with logical arguments (**9** 6–23). |
| He chides the warden, countering his argument about children (**9** 24–27). | Logical and moral argument in favour of control, appealing to a certain sense of responsibility (**9** 28–35). |

At this point the arguments cease, as neither man seems to have more to say. No solution is reached. At the end of the story, both characters reiterate their positions (**10** 7–10).

2. *What is the effect of the hider's remark, "The woods are beautiful tonight, aren't they?" (**10** 3)?*
It confirms the narrator's assumption that the two men had a lot in common and could have been good friends.

3. *Do you think the narrator really believes his own arguments? Is his final attempt to console the hider ("They're developing an olfactory unit..." **10** 10) convincing? Discuss.*

## 2. Characters

1. *Contrast the relationship between the narrator and Almack with the relationship between the narrator and the hider.*

a) *Narrator—Almack*: The relationship is distant and functional. The alienation between them is underlined by the physical distance created by the floater.

b) *Narrator—hider*: Their physical struggle is the opposite of the distanced interaction between the narrator and Almack. They share pain in both a physical and emotional sense. It may be useful for students to compare the conversations the narrator holds with Almack on the one hand and the hider on the other. Students could find references to illustrate a) and b).

*2. What do all three characters in the story have in common?*
They all want to protect the wilderness. One could say Almack and the hider represent two extreme views of how to attain this goal: one of them wishes to exclude human beings completely and give them access only via advanced technology. The other wants to see nature-lovers have full access to the wilderness. The narrator, it seems, is torn between these extremes.

# 3. For further discussion

*In which direction do you tend? Should people be excluded from wilderness areas, should they have partial access, or should they be allowed in without restrictions?*

# 4. Presentations

*1. Give a talk on the environmental effects of a recreational activity that is carried out in a natural setting, e.g. ski-ing, mountain-bike riding.*

*2. Find out about one national park in an English-speaking country: its foundation, characteristics, conditions for visitors (entrance fee? motor traffic?) and number of visitors per year. Present this information to your class, with the help of visual materials if possible.*

Daphne du Maurier

# The Birds

On December the third the wind changed overnight and it was winter. Until then the autumn had been mellow, soft. The earth was rich where the plough had turned it.

Nat Hocken, because of a wartime disability, had a pension and did not work full-time at the farm. He worked three days a week, and they gave him the lighter jobs. Although he was married, with children, his was a solitary disposition; he liked best to work alone.

It pleased him when he was given a bank to build up, or a gate to mend, at the far end of the peninsula, where the sea surrounded the farmland on either side. Then, at midday, he would pause and eat the meat pie his wife had baked for him and, sitting on the cliff's edge, watch the birds.

In autumn great flocks of them came to the peninsula, restless, uneasy, spending themselves in motion; now wheeling, circling in the sky; now settling to feed on the rich, new-turned soil; but even when they fed, it was as though they did so without hunger, without desire.

Restlessness drove them to the skies again. Crying, whistling, calling, they skimmed the placid sea and left the shore.

Make haste, make speed, hurry and begone; yet where, and to what purpose? The restless urge of autumn, unsatisfying, sad, had put a spell upon them, and they must spill themselves of motion before winter came.

Perhaps, thought Nat, a message comes to the birds in autumn, like a warning. Winter is coming. Many of them will perish. And like people who, apprehensive of death before their time, drive themselves to work or folly, the birds do likewise; tomorrow we shall die.

The birds had been more restless than ever this fall of the year, their agitation more remarked because the days were still.

---

2 **mellow** pleasant, with warm light – 7 **disposition** character – 8 **bank** *here:* raised ground along edge of water – 9 **to mend** to repair (clothes, fences) – 14 **motion** movement – 18 **to skim** to fly quickly over a surface, just touching it – **placid** ['plæsɪd] calm – 20 **urge** [ɜːdʒ] strong desire to act – **to put a spell upon s.o.** *jdn verzaubern* – 21 **to spill oneself of motion** to work off energy – 24 **to perish** to die – 26 **folly** foolishness

## 12 Daphne du Maurier, The Birds

As Mr Trigg's tractor traced its path up and down the western hills, and Nat, hedging, saw it dip and turn, the whole machine and the man upon it were momentarily lost in the great cloud of wheeling, crying birds.

Nat remarked upon them to Mr Trigg when the work was finished for the day.

"Yes," said the farmer, "there are more birds about than usual. I have a notion the weather will change. It will be a hard winter. That's why the birds are restless."

The farmer was right. That night the weather turned.

The bedroom in the cottage faced east. Nat woke just after two and heard the east wind, cold and dry. It sounded hollow in the chimney, and a loose slate rattled on the roof. Nat listened, and he could hear the sea roaring in the bay. He drew the blanket around him, leaned closer to the back of his wife, deep in sleep. Then he heard the tapping on the windowpane. It continued until, irritated by the sound, Nat got out of bed and went to the window. He opened it; and as he did so something brushed his hand, jabbing at his knuckles, grazing the skin. Then he saw the flutter of wings and the thing was gone again, over the roof, behind the cottage.

It was a bird. What kind of bird he could not tell. The wind must have driven it to shelter on the sill.

He shut the window and went back to bed, but feeling his knuckles wet, put his mouth to the scratch. The bird had drawn blood.

Frightened, he supposed, bewildered, seeking shelter, the bird had stabbed at him in the darkness. Once more he settled himself to sleep.

Presently the tapping came again—this time more forceful, more insistent. And now his wife woke at the sound and turning in the bed, said to him, "See to the window, Nat; it's rattling."

"I've already been to it," he told her. "There's some bird there, trying to get in."

"Send it away," she said. "I can't sleep with that noise."

He went to the window for the second time, and now when he opened it, there was not one bird on the sill but half a dozen; they flew straight into his face.

---

2 **to hedge** to cut or trim hedges – 18 **to jab at** *stechen* – **knuckle** ['nʌkl] *Fingerknöchel* – **to graze** to wound the skin by scraping it on s.th. – 22 **to shelter** to look for protection – 25 **bewildered** [bɪˈwɪldəd] confused – 27 **insistent** [-ˈ--] not stopping or giving up

## *Daphne du Maurier, The Birds*

He shouted, striking out at them with his arms, scattering them; like the first one, they flew over the roof and disappeared.

He let the window fall and latched it.

Suddenly a frightened cry came from the room across the passage where the children slept.

"It's Jill," said his wife, roused at the sound.

There came a second cry, this time from both children. Stumbling into their room, Nat felt the beating of wings about him in the darkness. The window was wide open. Through it came the birds, hitting first the ceiling and the walls, then swerving in mid-flight and turning to the children in their beds.

"It's all right. I'm here," shouted Nat, and the children flung themselves, screaming, upon him, while in the darkness the birds rose, and dived, and came for him again.

"What is it, Nat? What's happened?" his wife called. Swiftly he pushed the children through the door to the passage and shut it upon them, so that he was alone in their bedroom with the birds.

He seized a blanket from the nearest bed, and using it as a weapon, flung it to right and left about him.

He felt the thud of bodies, heard the fluttering of wings; but the birds were not yet defeated, for again and again they returned to the assault, jabbing his hands, his head, their little stabbing beaks sharp as pointed forks.

The blanket became a weapon of defence. He wound it about his head, and then in greater darkness, beat at the birds with his bare hands. He dared not stumble to the door and open it lest the birds follow him.

How long he fought with them in the darkness he could not tell; but at last the beating of the wings about him lessened, withdrew; and through the dense blanket he was aware of light.

He waited, listened; there was no sound except the fretful crying of one of the children from the bedroom beyond.

He took the blanket from his head and stared about him. The cold grey morning light exposed the room.

Dawn and the open window had called the living birds; the dead lay on the floor.

---

1 **to scatter** spread over a large area – 6 **to rouse** [raʊz] to waken – 10 **to swerve** to change direction suddenly – 20 **thud** dull, hollow sound made by a falling object – 22 **beak** [biːk] *Schnabel* – 26 **lest** in case *(aus Furcht, daß... )* – 29 **to withdraw** to go away again – 31 **fretful** worried

## 14 *Daphne du Maurier, The Birds*

Sickened, Nat went to the window and stared out across his patch of garden to the fields.

It was bitter cold, and the ground had all the hard, black look of the frost that the east wind brings. The sea, fiercer now with turning tide, whitecapped and steep, broke harshly in the bay. Of the birds there was no sign.

Nat shut the window and the door of the small bedroom and went back across the passage to his own room.

His wife sat up in bed, one child asleep beside her; the smaller one in her arms, his face bandaged.

"He's sleeping now," she whispered. "Something must have cut him; there was blood at the corners of his eyes. Jill said it was the birds. She said she woke up and the birds were in the room."

His wife looked up at Nat, searching his face for confirmation. She looked terrified, bewildered. He did not want her to know that he also was shaken, dazed almost, by the events of the past few hours.

"There are birds in there," he said. "Dead birds, nearly fifty of them. Robins, wrens, all of the little birds from here about. It's as though a madness seized them, with the east wind."

He sat down on the bed beside his wife, and held her hand.

"It's the hard weather," he said. "It must be that; it's the hard weather. They aren't the birds, maybe, from around here. They've been driven down from upcountry."

"But Nat," whispered his wife, "it's only this night that the weather turned. They can't be hungry yet. There's food for them out there in the fields."

"It's the weather," repeated Nat. "I tell you, it's the weather."

His face, too, was drawn and tired, like hers. They stared at one another for a while without speaking.

Nat went to the window and looked out. The sky was hard and leaden, and the brown hills that had gleamed in the sun the day before looked dark and bare. Black winter had descended in a single night.

The children were awake now. Jill was chattering, and young Johnny was crying once again. Nat heard his wife's voice, soothing, comforting them as he went downstairs.

Presently they came down. He had breakfast ready for them.

---

5 **harshly** with force – 14 **confirmation** a sign that s.th. is correct – 16 **to be dazed** to be unable to think clearly – 18 **robin** *Rotkehlchen* – **wren** [ren] *Zaunkönig* – 31 **leaden** ['lednˌ] *bleiern* – 32 **to descend** to come down – 34 **to soothe** [suːð] to calm – **to comfort** ['kʌmfət] to take away fear

"Did you drive away the birds?" asked Jill.

"Yes, they've all gone now," Nat said. "It was the east wind brought them in."

"I hope they won't come again," said Jill.

"I'll walk with you to the bus," Nat said to her.

Jill seemed to have forgotten her experience of the night before. She danced ahead of him, chasing the leaves, her face rosy under her pixie hood.

All the while Nat searched the hedgerows for the birds, glanced over them to the fields beyond, looked to the small wood above the farm where the rooks and jackdaws gathered; he saw none. Soon the bus came ambling up the hill.

Nat saw Jill onto the bus, then turned and walked back toward the farm. It was not his day for work, but he wanted to satisfy himself that all was well. He went to the back door of the farmhouse; he heard Mrs Trigg singing, the wireless making a background for her song.

"Are you there, missus?" Nat called.

She came to the door, beaming, broad, a good-tempered woman.

"Hullo, Mr Hocken," she said. "Can you tell me where this cold is coming from? Is it Russia? I've never seen such a change. And it's going on, the wireless says. Something to do with the Arctic Circle."

"We didn't turn on the wireless this morning," said Nat. "Fact is, we had trouble in the night."

"Kiddies poorly?"

"No." He hardly knew how to explain. Now, in daylight, the battle of the birds would sound absurd.

He tried to tell Mrs Trigg what had happened, but he could see from her eyes that she thought his story was the result of nightmare following a heavy meal.

"Sure they were real birds?" she said, smiling.

"Mrs Trigg," he said, "there are fifty dead birds, robins, wrens, and such, lying low on the floor of the children's bedroom. I suppose the weather brought them; once in the bedroom they went for me; they tried to go for young Johnny's eyes."

Mrs Trigg stared at him doubtfully. "Well, now," she answered. "I suppose the weather brought them; once in the bedroom they wouldn't know where they were. Foreign birds maybe, from that Arctic Circle."

---

7-8 **pixie hood** pointed woollen hat – 11 **rook** [rʊk] *Saatkrähe* – **jackdaw** *Dohle* – 12 **to amble** *here:* to move slowly – 18 **to beam** to smile broadly – 24 **poorly** not well

## 16 *Daphne du Maurier, The Birds*

"No," said Nat. "They were the birds you see about here every day."
"Funny thing," said Mrs Trigg. "No explaining it, really. You ought to write up and ask the *Guardian*. They'd have some answer for it. Well, I must be getting on."

Nat walked back along the lane to his cottage. He found his wife in the kitchen with young Johnny.

"See anyone?" she asked.

"Mrs Trigg," he answered. "I don't think she believed me. Anyway, nothing wrong up there."

"You might take the birds away," she said. "I daren't go into the room to make the beds until you do. I'm scared."

"Nothing to scare you now," said Nat. "They're dead, aren't they?"

He went up with a sack and dropped the stiff bodies into it, one by one. Yes, there were fifty of them all told. Just the ordinary, common birds of the hedgerow; nothing as large even as a thrush. It must have been fright that made them act the way they did.

He took the sack out into the garden and was faced with a fresh problem. The ground was frozen solid, yet no snow had fallen; nothing had happened in the past hours but the coming of the east wind. It was unnatural, queer. He could see the whitecapped seas breaking in the bay. He decided to take the birds to the shore and bury them.

When he reached the beach below the headland, he could scarcely stand, the force of the east wind was so strong. It was low tide; he crunched his way over the shingle to the softer sand and then, his back to the wind, opened up his sack.

He ground a pit in the sand with his heel, meaning to drop the birds into it; but as he did so, the force of the wind lifted them as though in flight again, and they were blown away from him along the beach, tossed like feathers, spread and scattered.

The tide will take them when it turns, he said to himself.

He looked out to sea and watched the crested breakers, combing green. They rose stiffly, curled, and broke again; and because it was ebb tide, the roar was distant, more remote, lacking the sound and thunder of the flood.

Then he saw them. The gulls. Out there, riding the seas.

---

15 **thrush** [θrʌʃ]*Drossel* – 20 **queer** strange, odd, peculiar – 22 **headland** a narrow piece of land protruding into the sea – 24 **shingle** [ˈʃɪŋgl] *Kiesel* – 26 **heel** back part of one's foot – 31 **crested** with a peak, like a mountain top – **breakers** large waves – **to comb** [kəʊm] to pull through in parallel lines – 33 **remote** far away – **to lack** not to have – 35 **gull** *Möwe*

*Daphne du Maurier, The Birds*

What he had thought at first were the whitecaps of the waves were gulls. Hundreds, thousands, tens of thousands.

They rose and fell in the troughs of the seas, heads to the wind, like a mighty fleet at anchor, waiting on the tide.

Nat turned; leaving the beach, he climbed the steep path home.

Someone should know of this. Someone should be told. Something was happening because of the east wind and the weather, that he did not understand.

As he drew near the cottage, his wife came to meet him at the door. She called to him, excited. "Nat," she said, "it's on the wireless. They've just read out a special news bulletin. It's not only here, it's everywhere. In London, all over the country. Something has happened to the birds. Come listen; they're repeating it."

Together they went into the kitchen to listen to the announcement.

"Statement from the Home Office, at eleven A.M. this morning. Reports from all over the country are coming in hourly about the vast quantity of birds flocking above towns, villages, and outlying districts, causing obstruction and damage and evening attacking individuals. It is thought that the Arctic air stream at present covering the British Isles is causing birds to migrate south in immense numbers, and that intense hunger may drive these birds to attack human beings. Householders are warned to see to their windows, doors, and chimneys, and to take reasonable precautions for the safety of their children. A further statement will be issued later."

A kind of excitement seized Nat. He looked at his wife in triumph. "There you are," he said. "I've been telling myself all morning there's something wrong. And just now, down on the beach, I looked out to sea and there were gulls, thousands of them, riding on the sea, waiting."

"What are they waiting for, Nat?" she asked.

He stared at her. "I don't know," he said slowly.

He went over to the drawer where he kept his hammer and other tools.

"What are you going to do, Nat?"

"See to the windows and the chimneys, like they tell you to."

"You think they would break in with the windows shut? Those wrens and robins and such? Why, how could they?"

---

3 **trough** [trɒf] the channel between two waves – 15 **Home Office** government department responsible for police, immigration and broadcasting – 17 **to flock** to gather in large numbers – 18 **obstruction** blockage – 23 **precautions** [-'--] safety measures

*18 Daphne du Maurier, The Birds*

He did not answer. He was not thinking of the robins and the wrens. He was thinking of the gulls.

He went upstairs and worked there the rest of the morning, boarding the windows of the bedrooms, filling up the chimney bases.

"Dinner's ready." His wife called from the kitchen.

"All right. Coming down."

When dinner was over and his wife was washing up, Nat switched on the one o'clock news. The same announcement was repeated, but the news bulletin enlarged upon it. "The flocks of birds have caused dislocation in all areas," said the announcer, "and in London the mass was so dense at ten o'clock this morning that it seemed like a vast black cloud. The birds settled on rooftops, on window ledges, and on chimneys. The species included blackbird, thrush, the common house sparrow, and as might be expected in the metropolis, a vast quantity of pigeons, starlings, and the frequenter of the London river, the black-headed gull. The sight was so unusual that traffic came to a standstill in many thoroughfares, work was abandoned in shops and offices, and the streets and pavements were crowded with people standing about to watch the birds."

The announcer's voice was smooth and suave; Nat had the impression that he treated the whole business as he would an elaborate joke. There would be others like him, hundreds of them, who did not know what it was to struggle in darkness with a flock of birds.

Nat switched off the wireless. He got up and started work on the kitchen windows. His wife watched him, young Johnny at her heels.

"What they ought to do," she said, "is to call the army out and shoot the birds."

"Let them try," said Nat. "How'd they set about it?"

"I don't know. But something should be done. They ought to do something."

Nat thought to himself that "they" were no doubt considering the problem at that very moment, but whatever "they" decided to do in London and the big cities would not help them here, nearly three hundred miles away.

"How are we off for food?" he asked.

"It's shopping day tomorrow, you know that. I don't keep uncooked

---

10 **dislocation** destruction of infrastructure – 13 **blackbird** *Amsel* – 14 **sparrow** *Spatz* – 15 **pigeon** *Taube* – **starling** *Star* – **frequenter** s.o. who is often in a certain place – 17 **thoroughfare** ['θʌrəfɛə] main road in a town or city – 20 **sauve** [swaːv] polished, charming – 21 **elaborate** [ɪ'læbərət] *here:* very clever and complex

food about. Butcher doesn't call till the day after. But I can bring back something when I go in tomorrow."

Nat did not want to scare her. He looked in the larder for himself and in the cupboard where she kept her tins.

They could hold out for a couple of days.

He went on hammering the boards across the kitchen windows. Candles. They were low on candles. That must be another thing she meant to buy tomorrow. Well, they must go early to bed tonight. That was, if—

He got up and went out the back door and stood in the garden, looking down toward the sea.

There had been no sun all day, and now, at barely three o'clock, a kind of darkness had already come; the sky was sullen, heavy, colourless like salt. He could hear the vicious sea drumming on the rocks.

He walked down the path halfway to the beach. And then he stopped. He could see the tide had turned. The gulls had risen. They were circling, hundreds of them, thousands of them, lifting their wings against the wind.

It was the gulls that made the darkening of the sky.

And they were silent. They just went on soaring and circling, rising, falling, trying their strength against the wind. Nat turned. He ran up the path back to the cottage.

"I'm going for Jill," he said to his wife.

"What's the matter?" she asked. "You've gone quite white."

"Keep Johnny inside," he said. "Keep the door shut. Light up now and draw the curtains."

"It's only gone three," she said.

"Never mind. Do what I tell you."

He looked inside the tool shed and took the hoe.

He started walking up the lane to the bus stop. Now and again he glanced back over his shoulder; and he could see the gulls had risen higher now, their circles were broader, they were spreading out in huge formation across the sky.

He hurried on. Although he knew the bus would not come before four o'clock, he had to hurry.

He waited at the top of the hill. There was half an hour still to go.

---

3 **larder** a room or cupboard in which food is kept – 13 **sullen** dull, unpleasant – 14 **vicious** ['vɪʃəs] brutal – 20 **to soar** [sɔə] to rise to great heights – 29 **shed** small building used for keeping things in – **hoe** *Hacke*

*Daphne du Maurier, The Birds*

The east wind came whipping across the fields from the higher ground. In the distance he could see the clay hills, white and clean against the heavy pallor of the sky.

Something black rose from behind them, like a smudge at first, then widening, becoming deeper. The smudge became a cloud; and the cloud divided again into five other clouds, spreading north, east, south, and west; and then they were not clouds at all but birds.

He watched them travel across the sky, within two or three hundred feet of him. He knew, from their speed, that they were bound inland; they had no business with the people here on the peninsula. They were rooks, crows, jackdaws, magpies, jays, all birds that usually preyed upon the smaller species, but bound this afternoon on some other mission.

He went to the telephone call box, stepped inside, lifted the receiver. The exchange would pass the message on. "I'm speaking from the highway," he said, "by the bus stop. I want to report large formations of birds travelling upcountry. The gulls are also forming in the bay."

"All right," answered the voice, laconic, weary.

"You'll be sure and pass this message on to the proper quarter?"

"Yes. Yes." Impatient now, fed up. The buzzing note resumed.

She's another, thought Nat. She doesn't care.

The bus came lumbering up the hill. Jill climbed out.

"What's the hoe for, Dad?"

"I just brought it along," he said. "Come on now, let's get home. It's cold; no hanging about. See how fast you can run."

He could see the gulls now, still silent, circling the fields, coming in toward the land.

"Look, Dad; look over there. Look at all the gulls."

"Yes. Hurry now."

"Where are they flying to? Where are they going?"

"Upcountry, I dare say. Where it's warmer."

He seized her hand and dragged her after him along the lane.

"Don't go so fast. I can't keep up."

The gulls were copying the rooks and the crows. They were spreading out, in formation, across the sky. They headed, in bands of thousands, to the four compass points.

---

2 **clay** heavy, fine soil *(Ton, Lehm)* – 3 **pallor** ['pælə] paleness – 5 **smudge** dirty spot – 11 **magpie** *Elster* – **jay** *Eichelhäher* – 12 **to prey upon** [preɪ] to hunt for food – **bound** *here:* aiming for a particular goal – 19 **quarter** *here:* person or department responsible – 20 **fed up** no longer able to tolerate s.th. – **to resume** to start again

*Daphne du Maurier, The Birds* 21

"Dad, what is it? What are the gulls doing?"

They were not intent upon their flight, as the crows, as the jackdaws, had been. They still circled overhead. Nor did they fly so high. It was as though they waited upon some signal; as though some decision had yet to be given.

"I wish the gulls would go away." Jill was crying. "I don't like them. They're coming closer to the lane."

He started running, swinging Jill after him. As they went past the farm turning, he saw the farmer backing his car into the garage. Nat called to him.

"Can you give us a lift?" he said.

Mr Trigg turned in the driver's seat and stared at them. Then a smile came to his cheerful, rubicund face. "It looks as though we're in for some fun," he said. "Have you seen the gulls? Jim and I are going to take a crack at them. Everyone's gone bird crazy, talking of nothing else. I hear you were troubled in the night. Want a gun?"

Nat shook his head.

The small car was packed, but there was room for Jill on the back seat.

"I don't want a gun," said Nat, "but I'd be obliged if you'd run Jill home. She's scared of the birds."

"Okay," said the farmer. "I'll take her home. Why don't you stop behind and join the shooting match? We'll make the feathers fly."

Jill climbed in, and turning the car, the driver sped up the lane. Nat followed after. Trigg must be crazy. What use was a gun against a sky of birds?

They were coming in now toward the farm, circling lower in the sky. The farm, then, was their target. Nat increased his pace toward his own cottage. He saw the farmer's car turn and come back along the lane. It drew up beside him with a jerk.

"The kid has run inside," said the farmer. "Your wife was watching for her. Well, what do you make of it? They're saying in town the Russians have done it. The Russians have poisoned the birds."

"How could they do that?" asked Nat.

"Don't ask me. You know how stories get around."

"Have you boarded your windows?" asked Nat.

"No. Lot of nonsense. I've had more to do today than to go around boarding up my windows."

---

13 **rubicund** ['ruːbikənd] red – 15 **to take a crack at s.th.** *here:* to try to shoot s.th. – 28 **target** ['tɑːgɪt] the point s.o. is aiming at – 30 **jerk** sudden movement

## 22 Daphne du Maurier, The Birds

"I'd board them now if I were you."
"Garn. You're windy. Like to come to our place to sleep?"
"No, thanks all the same."
"All right. See you in the morning. Give you a gull breakfast."

The farmer grinned and turned his car to the farm entrance. Nat hurried on. Past the little wood, past the old barn, and then across the stile to the remaining field. As he jumped the stile, he heard the whir of wings. A black-backed gull dived down at him from the sky. It missed, swerved in flight, and rose to dive again. In a moment it was joined by others—six, seven, a dozen.

Nat dropped his hoe. The hoe was useless. Covering his head with his arms, he ran toward the cottage.

They kept coming at him from the air—noiseless, silent, save for the beating wings. The terrible, fluttering wings. He could feel the blood on his hands, his wrists, upon his neck. If only he could keep them from his eyes. Nothing else mattered.

With each dive, with each attack, they became bolder. And they had no thought for themselves. When they dived low and missed, they crashed, bruised and broken, on the ground.

As Nat ran he stumbled, kicking their spent bodies in front of him. He found the door and hammered upon it with his bleeding hands. "Let me in," he shouted. "It's Nat. Let me in."

Then he saw the gannet, poised for the dive, above him in the sky.

The gulls circled, retired, soared, one with another, against the wind.

Only the gannet remained. One single gannet, above him in the sky. Its wings folded suddenly to its body. It dropped like a stone.

Nat screamed; and the door opened.

He stumbled across the threshold, and his wife threw her weight against the door.

They heard the thud of the gannet as it fell.

His wife dressed his wounds. They were not deep. The backs of his hands had suffered most, and his wrists. Had he not worn a cap, the birds would have reached his head. As for the gannet—the gannet could have split his skull.

The children were crying, of course. They had seen the blood on their father's hands.

---

2 **Garn** (*slang*) Go on – **windy** *here:* afraid – 7 **stile** step on both sides of a fence surrounding a field – 19 **to bruise** [bruːz] to injure a part of the body by a hard hit – 23 **gannet** large sea bird *(Tölpel)* – **to be poised** [pɔɪzd] to be positioned ready for s.th.

*Daphne du Maurier, The Birds* 23

"It's all right now," he told them. "I'm not hurt."

His wife was ashen. "I saw them overhead," she whispered. "They began collecting just as Jill ran in with Mr Trigg. I shut the door fast, and it jammed. That's why I couldn't open it at once when you came."

"Thank God the birds waited for me," he said. "Jill would have fallen at once. They're flying inland, thousands of them. Rooks, crows, all the bigger birds. I saw them from the bus stop. They're making for the towns."

"But what can they do, Nat?"

"They'll attack. Go for everyone out in the streets. Then they'll try the windows, the chimneys."

"Why don't the authorities do something? Why don't they get the army, get machine guns?"

"There's been no time. Nobody's prepared. We'll hear what they have to say on the six o'clock news."

"I can hear the birds," Jill said. "Listen, Dad."

Nat listened. Muffled sounds came from the windows, from the door. Wings brushing the surface, sliding, scraping, seeking a way of entry. The sound of many bodies pressed together, shuffling on the sills. Now and again came a thud, a crash, as some bird dived and fell.

Some of them will kill themselves that way, he thought, but not enough. Never enough.

"All right," he said aloud. "I've got boards over the windows, Jill. The birds can't get in."

He went and examined all the windows. He found wedges—pieces of old tin, strips of wood and metal—and fastened them at the sides of the windows to reinforce the boards.

His hammering helped to deafen the sound of the birds, the shuffling, the tapping, and—more ominous—the splinter of breaking glass.

"Turn on the wireless," he said.

He went upstairs to the bedrooms and reinforced the windows there. Now he could hear the birds on the roof—the scraping of claws, a sliding, jostling sound.

He decided the whole family must sleep in the kitchen and keep up the fire. He was afraid of the bedroom chimneys. The boards he had placed at their bases might give way. In the kitchen they would be safe because of the fire.

---

25 **wedge** object pushed between two other objects to make them fit tightly – 33 **to jostle** ['dʒɒsl] to bump into other objects or bodies

## 24 *Daphne du Maurier, The Birds*

He would have to make a joke of it. Pretend to the children they were playing camp. If the worst happened and the birds forced an entry by way of the bedroom chimneys, it would be hours, days perhaps, before they could break down the doors. The birds would be imprisoned in the bedrooms. They could do no harm there. Crowded together, they would stifle and die. He began to bring the mattresses downstairs.

At sight of them, his wife's eyes widened in apprehension.

"All right," he said cheerfully. "We'll all sleep together in the kitchen tonight. More cosy, here by the fire. Then we won't be worried by those silly old birds tapping at the windows."

He made the children help him rearrange the furniture, and he took the precaution of moving the dresser against the windows.

We're safe enough now, he thought. We're snug and tight. We can hold out. It's just the food that worries me. Food and coal for the fire. We've enough for two or three days, not more. By that time—

No use thinking ahead as far as that. And they'd be given directions on the wireless.

And now, in the midst of many problems, he realized that only dance music was coming over the air. He knew the reason. The usual programmes had been abandoned; this only happened at exceptional times.

At six o'clock the records ceased. The time signal was given. There was a pause, and then the announcer spoke. His voice was solemn, grave. Quite different from midday.

"This is London," he said. "A national emergency was proclaimed at four o'clock this afternoon. Measures are being taken to safeguard the lives and property of the population, but it must be understood that these are not easy to effect immediately, owing to the unforeseen and unparalleled nature of the present crisis. Every householder must take precautions about his own building. Where several people live together, as in flats and hotels, they must unite to do the utmost that they can to prevent entry. It is absolutely imperative that every individual stay indoors tonight.

"The birds, in vast numbers, are attacking anyone on sight, and have already begun an assault upon buildings; but these, with due care, should be impenetrable.

---

6 **to stifle** ['staɪfl] to run out of air – 8 **apprehension** fear that something terrible may happen – 10 **cosy** comfortable and warm – 13 **dresser** piece of furniture with shelves, drawers and cupboard space – 14 **snug** cosy – 21 **to abandon** [əˈbændən] to give up 24 **solemn** ['sɒləm] serious – 25 **grave** very serious, worried

"The population is asked to remain calm.

"Owing to the exceptional nature of the emergency, there will be no further transmission from any broadcasting station until seven A.M. tomorrow."

They played "God Save the Queen." Nothing more happened.

Nat switched off the set. He looked at his wife. She stared back at him.

"We'll have supper early," suggested Nat. "Something for a treat— toasted cheese, eh? Something we all like."

He winked and nodded at his wife. He wanted the look of dread, of apprehension, to leave her face.

He helped with the supper, whistling, singing, making as much clatter as he could. It seemed to him that the shuffling and the tapping were not so intense as they had been at first, and presently he went up to the bedrooms and listened. He no longer heard the jostling for place upon the roof.

They've got reasoning powers, he thought. They know it's hard to break in here. They'll try elsewhere.

Supper passed without incident. Then, when they were clearing away, they heard a new sound, a familiar droning.

His wife looked up at him, her face alight.

"It's planes," she said. "They're sending out planes after the birds. That will get them. Isn't that gunfire? Can't you hear guns?"

It might be gunfire, out at sea. Nat could not tell. Big naval guns might have some effect upon the gulls out at sea, but the gulls were inland now. The guns couldn't shell the shore because of the population.

"It's good, isn't it," said his wife, "to hear the planes?"

Catching her enthusiasm, Jill jumped up and down with Johnny. "The planes will get the birds."

Just then they heard a crash about two miles distant. Followed by a second, then a third. The droning became more distant, passed away out to sea.

"What was that?" asked his wife.

"I don't know," answered Nat. He did not want to tell her that the sound they had heard was the crashing of aircraft.

It was, he had no doubt, a gamble on the part of the authorities to send out reconnaissance forces, but they might have known the gam-

---

8 **treat** [triːt] s.th. special – 10 **dread** [dred] great fear – 31 **droning** sound made by aeroplanes – 36 **gamble** risky action or decision – 37 **reconnaissance** [rɪˈkɒnɪsəns] *Aufklärung*

## 26 *Daphne du Maurier, The Birds*

ble was suicidal. What could aircraft do against birds that flung themselves to death against propeller and fuselage but hurtle to the ground themselves?

"Where have the planes gone, Dad?" asked Jill.

"Back to base," he said. "Come on now, time to tuck down for bed."

There was no further drone of aircraft, and the naval guns had ceased. Waste of life and effort, Nat said to himself. We can't destroy enough of them that way. Cost too heavy. There's always gas. Maybe they'll try spraying with gas, mustard gas. We'll be warned first, of course, if they do. There's one thing, the best brains of the country will be on it tonight.

Upstairs in the bedrooms all was quiet. No more scraping and stabbing at the windows. A lull in battle. The wind hadn't dropped, though. Nat could still hear it roaring in the chimneys. And the sea breaking down on the shore.

Then he remembered the tide. The tide would be on the turn. Maybe the lull in battle was because of the tide. There was some law the birds obeyed, and it had to do with the east wind and the tide.

He glanced at his watch. Nearly eight o'clock. It must have gone high water an hour ago. That explained the lull. The birds attacked with the flood tide.

He reckoned the time limit in his head. They had six hours to go without attack. When the tide turned again, around 1:20 in the morning, the birds would come back.

He called softly to his wife and whispered to her that he would go out and see how they were faring at the farm, see if the telephone was still working there so that they might get news from the exchange.

"You're not to go," she said at once, "and leave me alone with the children. I can't stand it."

"All right," he said, "all right. I'll wait till morning. And we can get the wireless bulletin then, too, at seven. But when the tide ebbs again, I'll try for the farm; they may let us have bread and potatoes."

His mind was busy again, planning against emergency. They would not have milked, of course, this evening. The cows would be standing by the gate, waiting; the household would be inside, battened behind boards as they were here at the cottage.

That is, if they had time to take precautions.

---

2 **fuselage** ['fjuːzɪlɑːʒ] *Flugzeugrumpf* – 13 **lull** pause in a storm or battle – 27 **exchange** *here:* building in which telephone calls are connected – 35 **to be battened** *here:* to be protected

*Daphne du Maurier, The Birds* 27

Softly, stealthily, he opened the back door and looked outside.

It was pitch-dark. The wind was blowing harder than ever, coming in steady gusts, icy, from the sea.

He kicked at the step. It was heaped with birds. These were the suicides, the divers, the ones with broken necks. Wherever he looked, he saw dead birds. The living had flown seaward with the turn of the tide. The gulls would be riding the seas now, as they had done in the forenoon.

In the far distance on the hill, something was burning. One of the aircraft that had crashed; the fire, fanned by the wind, had set light to a stack.

He looked at the bodies of the birds. He had a notion that if he stacked them, one upon the other, on the wind sills, they would be added protection against the next attack.

Not much, perhaps, but something. The bodies would have to be clawed at, pecked and dragged aside before the living birds gained purchase on the sills and attacked the panes.

He set to work in the darkness. It was queer. He hated touching the dead birds, but he went on with his work. He noticed grimly that every window pane was shattered. Only the boards had kept the birds from breaking in.

He stuffed the cracked panes with the bleeding bodies of the birds and felt his stomach turn. When he had finished, he went back into the cottage and barricaded the kitchen door, making it doubly secure.

His wife had made him cocoa; he drank it thirstily. He was very tired. "All right," he said, smiling, "don't worry. We'll get through."

He lay down on his mattress and closed his eyes.

He dreamed uneasily because, through his dreams, ran the dread of something forgotten. Some piece of work that he should have done. It was connected, in some way, with the burning aircraft.

It was his wife, shaking his shoulder, who awoke him finally.

They've begun," she sobbed. "They've started this last hour. I can't listen to it any longer alone. There's something smells bad too, something burning."

Then he remembered. He had forgotten to make up the fire.

The fire was smoldering, nearly out. He got up swiftly and lighted the lamp.

---

11 **stack** large pile of hay – 16-17 **to gain purchase** ['pɜːtʃəs] *here:* to get a hold on – 17 **pane** flat sheet of glass in a window – 19 **grimly** with anxiety

## 28 Daphne du Maurier, The Birds

The hammering had started at the windows and the door, but it was not that he minded now. It was the smell of singed feathers.

The smell filled the kitchen. He knew what it was at once. The birds were coming down the chimney, squeezing their way down to the kitchen range.

He got sticks and paper and put them on the embers, then reached for the can of kerosene.

"Stand back," he shouted to his wife. He threw some of the kerosene onto the fire.

The flame roared up the pipe, and down into the fire fell the scorched, blackened bodies of the birds.

The children waked, crying. "What is it?" asked Jill. "What's happened?"

Nat had no time to answer her. He was raking the bodies from the chimney, clawing them out onto the floor.

The flames would drive away the living birds from the chimney top. The lower joint was the difficulty though. It was choked with the smoldering, helpless bodies of the birds caught by fire.

He scarcely heeded the attack on the windows and the door. Let them beat their wings, break their backs, lose their lives, in the desperate attempt to force an entry into his home. They would not break in.

"Stop crying," he called to the children. "There's nothing to be afraid of. Stop crying."

He went on raking out the burning, smoldering bodies as they fell into the fire.

This'll fetch them, he said to himself. The draught and the flames together. We're all right as long as the chimney doesn't catch.

Amid the tearing at the window boards came the sudden homely striking of the kitchen clock. Three o'clock.

A little more than four hours to go. He could not be sure of the exact time of high water. He reckoned the tide would not turn much before half past seven.

He waited by the range. The flames were dying. But no more blackened bodies fell from the chimney. He thrust his poker up as far as it could go and found nothing.

---

2 **to singe** [sɪndʒ] to burn s.th. slightly without it catching fire – 5 **range** *here:* stove – 6 **embers** small, glowing pieces of wood or coal that remain after fire – 11 **to be scorched** to be burnt on the surface – 14 **to rake** *rechen* – 19 **to heed** to pay attention to – 27 **to fetch** *here:* to get rid of – **draught** [drɑːft] air flowing strongly in one direction

*Daphne du Maurier, The Birds* 29

The danger of the chimney's being choked up was over. It could not happen again, not if the fire was kept burning day and night.

I'll have to get more fuel from the farm tomorrow, he thought. I can do all that with the ebb tide. It can be worked; we can fetch what we need when the tide's turned. We've just got to adapt ourselves, that's all.

They drank tea and cocoa, ate slices of bread. Only half a loaf left, Nat noticed. Never mind, though; they'd get by.

If they could hang on like this until seven, when the first news bulletin came through, they would not have done too badly.

"Give us a smoke," he said to his wife. "It will clear away the smell of the scorched feathers."

"There's only two left in the packet," she said. "I was going to buy you some."

"I'll have one," he said.

He sat with one arm around his wife and one around Jill, with Johnny on his lap, the blankets heaped about them on the mattress.

"You can't help admiring the beggars," he said. "They've got persistency. You'd think they'd tire of the game, but not a bit of it."

Admiration was hard to sustain. The tapping went on and on; and a new, rasping note struck Nat's ear, as though a sharper beak than any hitherto had come to take over from its fellows.

He tried to remember the names of birds; he tried to think which species would go for this particular job.

It was not the tap of the woodpecker. That would be light and frequent. This was more serious; if it continued long, the wood would splinter as the glass had done.

Then he remembered the hawks. Could the hawks have taken over from the gulls? Were there buzzards now upon the sills, using talons as well as beaks? Hawks, buzzards, kestrels, falcons; he had forgotten the birds of prey. He had forgotten the gripping power of the birds of prey. Three hours to go; and while they waited, the sound of the splintering wood, the talons tearing at the wood.

Nat looked about him, seeing what furniture he could destroy to fortify the door.

---

18 **persistency** will to keep going – 20 **to sustain** [sə'steɪn] to keep up – 21 **to rasp** to sound as if s.th is being rubbed on an uneven surface – 22 **hitherto** [hɪðə'tu:] up to now – 25 **woodpecker** *Specht* – 28 **hawk** *Habicht* – 29 **buzzard** ['bʌzəd] – **talon** claw of a bird of prey – 30 **kestrel** *Turmfalke*

## 30 *Daphne du Maurier, The Birds*

The windows were safe because of the dresser. He was not certain of the door. He went upstairs; but when he reached the landing, he paused and listened.

There was a soft patter on the floor of the children's bedroom. The birds had broken through.

The other bedroom was still clear. He brought out the furniture to pile at the head of the stairs should the door of the children's bedroom go.

"Come down, Nat. What are you doing?" called his wife.

"I won't be long," he shouted. "I'm just making everything shipshape up here."

He did not want her to come. He did not want her to hear the pattering in the children's bedroom, the brushing of those wings against the door.

After he suggested breakfast, he found himself watching the clock, gazing at the hands that went so slowly around the dial. If his theory was not correct, if the attack did not cease with the turn of the tide, he knew they were beaten. They could not continue through the long day without air, without rest, without fuel.

A crackling in his ears drove away the sudden, desperate desire for sleep.

"What is it? What now?" he said sharply.

"The wireless," said his wife. "I've been watching the clock. It's nearly seven."

The comfortable crackling of the wireless brought new life.

They waited. The kitchen clock struck seven.

The crackling continued. Nothing else. No chimes. No music.

They waited until a quarter past. No news bulletin came through.

"We heard wrong," he said. "They won't be broadcasting until eight o'clock."

They left the wireless switched on. Nat thought of the battery, wondered how much power was left in the battery. If it failed, they would not hear the instructions.

"It's getting light," whispered his wife. "I can't see it but I can feel it. And listen! The birds aren't hammering so loud now."

She was right. The rasping, tearing sound grew fainter every moment. So did the shuffling, the jostling for place upon the step, upon the sills. The tide was on the turn.

---

10 **shipshape** neat and tidy – 27 **chime** sound of a bell being struck once

*Daphne du Maurier, The Birds* 31

By eight there was no sound at all. Only the wind. And the crackling of the wireless. The children, lulled at last by the stillness, fell asleep.

At half past eight Nat switched the wireless off.

"We'll miss the news," said his wife.

"There isn't going to be any news," said Nat. "We've got to depend upon ourselves."

He went to the door and slowly pulled away the barricades. He drew the bolts, and kicking the broken bodies from the step outside the door, breathed the cold air.

He had six working hours before him, and he knew he must reserve his strength to the utmost, not waste it in any way.

Food and light and fuel; these were the most necessary things. If he could get them, they could endure another night.

He stepped into the garden; and as he did so, he saw the living birds. The gulls had gone to ride the sea, as they had done before. They sought sea food and the buoyancy of the tide before they returned to the attack.

Not so the land birds. They waited, and watched.

Nat saw them on the hedgerows, on the soil, crowded in the trees, outside in the field—line upon line of birds, still, doing nothing. He went to the end of his small garden.

The birds did not move. They merely watched him.

I've got to get food, Nat said to himself. I've got to go to the farm to get food.

He went back to the cottage. He saw to the windows and the door.

"I'm going to the farm," he said.

His wife clung to him. She had seen the living birds from the open door.

"Take us with you," she begged. "We can't stay here alone. I'd rather die than stay here alone."

"Come on, then," he said. "Bring baskets and Johnny's pram. We can load up the pram."

They dressed against the biting wind. His wife put Johnny in the pram, and Nat took Jill's hand.

"The birds," Jill whimpered. "They're all out there in the fields."

"They won't hurt us," he said. "Not in the light."

---

9 **bolt** metal bar that slides across to fasten the door – 17 **buoyancy** ['bɔɪənsɪ] *here: Tragfähigkeit* – 28 **to cling** to hold on tightly – 33 **pram** baby's bed on wheels

## 32 Daphne du Maurier, The Birds

They started walking across the field toward the stile, and the birds did not move. They waited, their heads turned to the wind.

When they reached the turning to the farm, Nat stopped and told his wife to wait in the shelter of the hedge with the two children. "But I want to see Mrs Trigg," she protested. "There are lots of things we can borrow if they went to market yesterday, and—"

"Wait here," Nat interrupted. "I'll be back in a moment."

The cows were lowing, moving restlessly in the yard, and he could see a gap in the fence where the sheep had knocked their way through to roam unchecked in the front garden before the farmhouse.

No smoke came from the chimneys. Nat was filled with misgiving. He did not want his wife or the children to go down to the farm.

He went down alone, pushing his way through the herd of lowing cows, who turned this way and that, distressed, their udders full.

He saw the car standing by the gate. Not put away in the garage. All the windows of the farmhouse were smashed. There were many dead gulls lying in the yard and around the house.

The living birds perched on the group of trees behind the farm and on the roof of the house. They were quite still. They watched him. Jim's body lay in the yard. What was left of it. His gun was beside him.

The door of the house was shut and bolted, but it was easy to push up a smashed window and climb through.

Trigg's body was close to the telephone. He must have been trying to get through to the exchange when the birds got him. The receiver was off the hook, and the instrument was torn from the wall.

No sign of Mrs Trigg. She would be upstairs. Was it any use going up? Sickened, Nat knew what he would find there.

Thank God, he said to himself, there were no children.

He forced himself to climb the stairs, but halfway up he turned and descended again. He could see Mrs Trigg's legs protruding from the open bedroom door. Beside her were the bodies of black-backed gulls and an umbrella, broken. It's no use doing anything, Nat thought. I've only got five hours; less than that. The Triggs would understand. I must load up with what I can find.

He tramped back to his wife and children.

"I'm going to fill up the car with stuff," he said. "We'll take it home and return for a fresh load."

"What about the Triggs?" asked his wife.

---

8 **to low** [ləʊ] to make a deep sound – 11 **misgiving** doubt and worry – 14 **to be distressed** to be very upset – **udder** Euter – 36 **stuff** (slang) various objects

*Daphne du Maurier, The Birds* 33

"They must have gone to friends," he said.

"Shall I come and help you then?"

"No, there's a mess down there. Cows and sheep all over the place. Wait; I'll get the car. You can sit in the car."

Her eyes watched his all the time he was talking. He believed she understood. Otherwise she certainly would have insisted on helping him find the bread and groceries.

They made three journeys altogether, to and from the farm, before he was satisfied they had everything they needed. It was surprising, once he started thinking, how many things were necessary. Almost the most important of all was planking for the windows. He had to go around searching for timber. He wanted to renew the boards on all the windows at the cottage.

On the final journey he drove the car to the bus stop and got out and went to the telephone box.

He waited a few minutes, jangling the hook. No good, though. The line was dead. He climbed onto a bank and looked over the countryside, but there was no sign of life at all, nothing in the fields but the waiting, watching birds.

Some of them slept; he could see their beaks tucked into their feathers.

You'd think they'd be feeding, he said to himself, not just standing that way.

Then he remembered. They were gorged with food. They had eaten their fill during the night. That was why they did not move this morning.

He lifted his face to the sky. It was colourless, grey. The bare trees looked bent and blackened by the east wind.

The cold did not affect the living birds, waiting out there in the fields.

This is the time they ought to get them, Nat said to himself. They're a sitting target now. They must be doing this all over the country. Why don't our aircraft take off now and spray them with mustard gas? What are all our chaps doing? They must know; they must see for themselves.

He went back to the car and got into the driver's seat.

---

11 **planking** boards of wood –12 **timber** wood used for building – 16 **to jangle s.th.** to move s.th. up and down – 24 **to be gorged with food** to have eaten an enormous amount – 33 **mustard gas** *Senfgas*

## 34 *Daphne du Maurier, The Birds*

"Go quickly past that second gate," whispered his wife. "The postman's lying there. I don't want Jill to see."

It was a quarter to one by the time they reached the cottage. Only an hour to go.

"Better have dinner," said Nat. "Heat up something for yourself and the children, some of that soup. I've no time to eat now. I've got to unload all this stuff from the car."

He got everything inside the cottage. It could be sorted later. Give them all something to do during the long hours ahead.

First he must see to the windows and the door.

He went around the cottage methodically, testing every window and the door. He climbed onto the roof also, and fixed boards across every chimney except the kitchen's.

The cold was so intense he could hardly bear it, but the job had to be done. Now and again he looked up, searching the sky for aircraft. None came. As he worked, he cursed the inefficiency of the authorities.

He paused, his work on the bedroom chimney finished, and looked out to sea. Something was moving out there. Something grey and white among the breakers.

"Good old navy," he said. "They never let us down. They're coming down channel; they're turning into the bay."

He waited, straining his eyes toward the sea. He was wrong, though. The navy was not there. It was the gulls rising from the sea. And the massed flocks in the fields with ruffled feathers, rose in formation from the ground and, wing to wing, soared upward to the sky.

The tide had turned again.

Nat climbed down the ladder and went inside the cottage. The family were at dinner. It was a little after two.

He bolted the door, put up the barricade, and lighted the lamp.

"It's night-time," said young Johnny.

His wife had switched on the wireless once again. The crackling sound came, but nothing else.

"I've been all around the dial," she said, "foreign stations and all. I can't get anything but the crackling."

"Maybe they have the same trouble," he said. "Maybe it's the same right through Europe."

They ate in silence.

16 **to curse** [kɜːs] *fluchen* – 25 **ruffled** *aufgeplustert*

*Daphne du Maurier, The Birds*

The tapping began at the windows, at the doors, the rustling, the jostling, the pushing for position on the sills. The first thud of the suicide gulls upon the step.

When he had finished dinner, Nat planned, he would put the supplies away, stack them neatly, get everything shipshape. The boards were strong against the windows and across the chimneys. The cottage was filled with stores, with fuel, with all they needed for the next few days.

His wife could help him, and the children too. They'd tire themselves out between now and a quarter to nine, when the tide would ebb; then he'd tuck them down on their mattresses, see that they slept good and sound until three in the morning.

He had a new scheme for the windows, which was to fix barbed wire in front of the boards. He had brought a great roll of it from the farm. The nuisance was, he'd have to work at this in the dark, when the lull came between nine and three. Pity he had not thought of it before. Still, as long as the wife and kids slept—that was the main thing.

The smaller birds were at the windows now. He recognized the light tap-tapping of their beaks and the soft brush of their wings.

The hawks ignored the windows. They concentrated their attack upon the door.

Nat listened to the tearing sound of splintering wood, and wondered how many million years of memory were stored in those little brains, behind the stabbing beaks, the piercing eyes, now giving them this instinct to destroy mankind with all the deft precision of machines.

"I'll smoke that last cigarette," he said to his wife. "Stupid of me. It was the one thing I forgot to bring back from the farm."

He reached for it, switched on the crackling wireless.

He threw the empty packet onto the fire and watched it burn.

---

11 **to tuck down** to put to bed comfortably – 13-14 **barbed wire** *Stacheldraht* – 15 **nuisance** ['nju:sns] annoyance – 22 **to tear** [teə] to rip – 24 **to stab** to attack with a sharp object – **to pierce** to penetrate with a sharp object – 25 **deft** skilful and quick

## Biographical Notes

*DAPHNE DU MAURIER (1907–1989), whose ancestors emigrated from France to England, was the granddaughter of a novelist and the daughter of a famous actor. She herself was an extremely successful writer, author of the bestsellers* Rebecca *and* The King's General. *The wild weather and countryside of Cornwall provide the setting for most of Daphne du Maurier's stories. Alfred Hitchcock's famous film* The Birds *is based on our story.*

# Summary and Teaching Notes

## Summary

Nat Hocken and his family live in a lonely cottage by the sea. One day in December, icy cold winter weather sets in, and the sea birds show signs of restlessness. That night birds unexpectedly attack Nat's home. All night long he fights off the birds, till dawn brings a respite. After seeing his daughter Jill off to school, Nat meets his neighbour's wife, Mrs Trigg, to whom he relates the night's events, but she fails to believe him.

When he returns home, a radio announcement informs listeners of an invasion of birds, probably due to the cold weather, and urges people to take precautions. A second announcement in the early afternoon confirms that the bird invasion is causing widespread damage and the situation is serious. This convinces Nat that he should check and strengthen his defences.

Then later in the afternoon, the gulls rise in their thousands. As Nat goes to fetch Jill at the bus-stop, they meet their neighbour, Mr Trigg, who treats the invasion as a huge joke. While Mr Trigg takes Jill home in his car, Nat follows on foot. Suddenly the birds attack him, and he rushes indoors just in time. Nat decides that the family will sleep in the kitchen. He does all he can to reassure them. The six o'clock news proclaims a state of national emergency, for the invasion is turning into a calamity. While Nat and his family settle down to supper the intensity of the attack seems to lessen. Their hopes are raised when they hear the sound of planes and gunfire. But the planes are heard to crash; the gunfire also ceases.

Then follows a lull, which Nat attributes to a turn in the tide. While he is trying to get some sleep he is awakened as birds attempt to come down the chimney. A fire fights them off.

Nat realizes that he needs to stock food. While everyone is waiting anxiously for daybreak, the birds renew their suicidal assaults. Suddenly Nat is aware that hawks have joined the fray. This is more serious.

At seven a.m. they switch on the radio; there is no news. The third attack ceases, the tide has turned. With six hours respite ahead of them the family set off for the farm to obtain food and supplies. Nat goes ahead and makes a gruesome discovery: the Triggs and the postman have been killed by the birds. The family make three journeys, laden with food and carrying planking to seal the windows.

Nat prepares to withstand another siege. At about 2 p.m. the tide turns, and masses of birds rise and fly inland. Nat barricades his cottage. Again there is no news.

The birds attack with increasing ferocity. They hack at the windows and the doors. Wondering why the birds should be so relentless in their destructive instincts, Nat smokes his last cigarette. The story ends here, and the outcome is left up to the reader's imagination.

# Teaching Notes

## 1. Structure

For the purposes of this interpretation, the story can be divided into five parts.

### I  A mere change of weather (11 1–12 10)

After reading this passage the students can be asked to consider how much they know about the setting of the story, the characters and the atmosphere that is created.

**Setting**
*Place:* an isolated farm at the far end of a peninsula where the sea surrounds the farmland on either side. There are hills to the west and a cliff facing the sea.
*Time:* late autumn, the first days of December. Students should note that the first and the last sentence of the introduction express exactly the same mood. In this way the author lays the stress on the significant nature of the change in the weather: from "mellow, soft" autumn (**11** 2) to "a hard winter" (**12** 8).

**Characters**
*Nat Hocken* is the main character. The reader is given various details about him. Because of a war-time disability he does not work full-time and is given lighter jobs. Nat is married with two children. He prefers to be alone. He likes watching the birds, meditating on them and comparing them to people ("Many of them will perish ... tomorrow we shall die" **11** 24, 26). At the time of the story's opening Nat notices that the birds have been more restless than ever this autumn.
*Mr Trigg* is Nat's employer, a forthright and plain-spoken farmer. He gives a matter-of-fact explanation for the birds' restlessness, but even as Nat watches him he is "momentarily lost in the great cloud of wheeling, crying birds" (**12** 3–4). This may be interpreted as a forewarning.

**Atmosphere**
An atmosphere of anxiety is created straight away: the sudden coming of winter in the opening sentence—brief, to the point, ending with the key word "winter". This contrasts with a mild autumn ("mellow", "soft", "rich"). The birds are unusually "restless, uneasy". Their motion seems to suggest an unsatisfied instinct, or yearning for something that remains inexplicable. The autumn seems to have affected them in an ominous way. The author uses words such as "sad" (**11** 20–21), "spell" (**11** 20), and "apprehensive of death" (**11** 25) to add tension.

**Suggested homework**
*Read the story as far as* **14** 32 *and write a summary of the night's events.*
These introductory paragraphs set the scene for us. As yet, nothing has happened. Provided students have neither read the rest of the story nor seen the film of it, they could try to invent a plot (in note form, in pairs perhaps) that could follow.


**II The first attack (12 1–14 32)**

A number of students should be asked to read their summaries aloud, for comparison and discussion. The discussion should bring out the relationship that exists between Nat's mounting irritation, turning to real anger and hatred, and the birds' increasing aggressiveness:

| *Nat* | *Birds* |
|---|---|
| Irritated by the tapping sound of birds. | |
| | They flutter away. |
| | More forceful, more insistent tapping. |
| | The birds fly straight into his face. |
| He shouts, striking at them. | |
| | The birds attack the children. |

He uses the blanket as a weapon.

                                    Again and again they return to their assault.

He beats at the birds with his bare hands.

                                    The dead birds lie on the ground.

## The aftermath of the battle

*1. Describe the scene and discuss how the characters feel about the night's terrifying events. How do they explain these events to one another?*

*The scene*

There is no sound except the crying of one of the children. Nearly fifty dead birds are in the children's room. The morning light is grey and cold. (**13** 33–34). Black winter has descended (**14** 32, cf. introduction). The frost has a "black look" (**14** 3); the sea is "fiercer now" (**14** 4). The increasing harshness of the setting reflects the increasing threat from the birds.

*Feelings*

Nat's wife is terrified, bewildered. Nat feels the same. He holds her hand, an instinctive gesture of the search for support, comfort, encouragement. She whispers, showing her fear and apprehension. His face is drawn and tired. They stare at each other without speaking (**14** 28–29). This emphasizes their anxiety. Whereas Nat's wife speaks openly of her fear, Nat tries to explain away the phenomenon of the birds by referring to the weather.

*2. Examine the last paragraph of this section ("Nat went to the window..." **14** 30–32). Pick out the words that lend a particularly ominous touch to the description. These are Nat's impressions of the landscape. Explain how they relate to his and his wife's feelings.*

– the "hard and leaden" sky. Normally such adjectives refer to solid material. The sky has become, against the laws of nature, its opposite.

– The "dark and bare" hills are contrasted with their previous bright appearance.
– "black winter". Again this is a seeming contradiction, an "unnatural" phenomenon. The phrase is aptly used by the author in order to stress the unusual and hostile atmosphere. We know that winter is associated with white snow, but here "black"—an apparent paradox—refers to black clouds, long dark nights and, by extension, to more dismal types of feelings. The distortion of the Hockens' natural surroundings corresponds to the distorted behaviour of the birds (" 'It's as though a madness seized them' " **14** 18–19). Nat and his wife sense that "black winter" encompasses far more than the weather.

*3. Comment on the style of* **12** 33–**13** 3.
These lines are dominated by the repetition of "He". This is a stylistic device to emphasize that the reader is perceiving the situation through Nat's eyes alone: a classic example of a limited point of view. The narrator is outside the story but limits the reader's vision to the thoughts and experiences of one character. Nat is also the most active character in the story. His wife, who remains nameless, is largely passive.

**Suggested homework**
*Read the story as far as* **22** 4 *and write a list of all the images related to war.*


**III The hours of anxiety** (**14** 33–**22** 4)

Having prepared the text the students should be able to appreciate the quality of the narrative parts, the aptness of the dialogues and the nature of the radio announcements. They should understand that despite the apparent ease in tension on the morning after the battle, suspense is growing.

*1. How do Nat and his wife react to the new situation?*
The sudden sighting of the gulls (**16** 35) marks a turning point (see "Style" below). Nat feels instinctively that the gulls are a greater threat to him and his family than the small birds he has just tried to bury. It is now that Nat decides to build up the defences around his house. He realizes that he must act by himself, whatever action "they", the au-

thorities in the big cities, may be taking. He proves to be independent, matching his "solitary disposition".

*2. What are Nat's main concerns?*
– to protect the windows (**17** 35)
– to obtain a supply of food and candles (**18** 35)
– Jill's security (**19** 23)

Nat feels mildly excited because his feelings and conclusions about the night's unusual events have been confirmed: he looks at his wife in triumph (**17** 25).

In the following passage Nat's wife asks her husband a number of questions which mirror the reader's possible questions:
– What are they waiting for? (**17** 30)
– What are you going to do? (**17** 34)
– You think they would break in with the windows shut?... Why, how could they? (**17** 36–37)

This literary device is frequently used to draw attention to a particular point. One character deliberately asks a question so as to elicit an answer that will inform the reader.

*3. How do other people react to the unusual situation?*
– *People in London* seem to be content merely to observe the phenomenon, with amused detachment.
– *The phone operator* is simply annoyed at the many calls she has to answer.
– *Mr Trigg* seems unconcerned. He does not take the events seriously. He treats them as a joke. He grins and smiles, looking forward even to an enjoyable shooting match and a full breakfast.

4. *List features of the style in* **16** *35–***17** *4. These lines represent a turning-point in the story.*
– three short remarks for dramatic effect, indicating surprise
– a comparison: white caps and gulls: similar colour, up-and-down movement with the waves
– rapid increase in numbers to suggest myriads, countless numbers, a vivid impression
– A longer, more rhythmic sentence ends the description. This rhythm should be emphasized, the sentence read aloud, like scanned poetry, for it suggests the rise and fall and rolling of the sea.

*Images of war*
- a mighty fleet at anchor (**17** 4)
- in huge formation (**19** 32–33)
- bound ... on some other mission (**20** 12–13)
- large formations of birds (**20** 16–17)
- waited upon some signal, as though some decision had yet to be given (**21** 4–5)
- the farm ... was their target (**21** 28)

Apart from the first image, all refer to planes at war. Images of war are used as a *leitmotif*: cf. Part II (attack, assault, weapon, defence, etc. ) and Part IV, where the attacks of the birds remind Nat of the air raids in World War II. The suicide birds (p. 22) recall the German *Stukas* and the Japanese *kamikaze* planes.


## IV A new attack and a lull in battle (**22** 5–**27** 30)

### The function of sounds during the attack
A possible approach to this unit lies in an analysis of the use of words which describe various sounds. Thus the student can perceive how the sounds made by the birds add to the increasing tension, emphasizing their aggressiveness:
- the whir of wings (**22** 7–8)
- noiseless, silent (**22** 13)
- beating wings; terrible, fluttering wings (**22** 14)
- they heard a thud (**22** 31)
- muffled sounds (**23** 17)
- brushing, sliding, scraping, shuffling, a thud, a crash (**23** 18–20)
- tapping, the splinter of breaking glass (**23** 29)
- the scraping of claws, a sliding jostling sound (**23** 32–33)
- the shuffling and the tapping (**25** 13)

It is also important to study the function and purpose of the other sounds, such as Nat's hammering, which helps to deafen the sound of the birds, the wireless broadcasting, dance music, the time signal, the solemn voice of the announcer. Then Nat whistles and sings, making as much clatter as he can; then we hear the familiar droning of aeroplanes, distant gunfire and three aeroplanes crashing.

**The lull in battle**
Suddenly everything is quiet; only the wind and the sea can still be heard (**26** 12–15).

*1. What role does the tide play in the story? How does it contribute to the suspense?*

"There was some law the birds obeyed..." (**26** 17–18). This law follows a natural pattern, i.e. the tides, but the behaviour of the birds is highly "unnatural, queer" (**16** 20). Is this law a law of nature? The tides introduce an element of hope to the story in that each "lull in battle" (**26** 13) allows Nat and his family to gain ground on the birds. Yet the tide tyrannizes the family, dictating their lives to them. Suspense is heightened by the race to beat the tide and by the increasing ferocity of the birds with each high tide.

*2. How does Nat use the time provided by the lull in the battle? What are his main concerns?*

*3. What would he have liked to do? Why doesn't he do it?*


**V The end** (**27** 31–end)

After the students have read the story to the end, they may be asked to explain the following quotations in order to provide a summary of the contents and to offer an interpretation at the same time:
– "You can't help admiring the beggars" (**29** 18).
Despite the apparently hopeless situation, Nat is able to give credit to the birds for their persistence, without, however, forgetting to make plans of how to "get by". Find examples of Nat's perseverance and resourcefulness.
– "He had forgotten the gripping power of the birds of prey" (**29** 31–32).
Nat is suddenly reminded of the seriousness of the situation when he realizes which type of bird makes this new, rasping sound. To Nat there is something foreboding and even evil about this type of bird, with their sudden presence at this stage.
– "He had six working hours before him" (**31** 11).

At this point in the story the students should have understood the role of the tide and ought to refer now to its influence on the birds, and their habits, which may be guided by the law of nature. Nat makes an attempt at obtaining the basic necessities to sustain another night's siege: fuel, light, food.
- "What about the Triggs?" (**32** 38).
- "They must have gone to friends" (**33** 1).

Nat is filled with misgivings and does not want his wife and children to know what has happened. In fact, before he discovers the bodies he knows that the Triggs cannot have survived because of Mr Trigg's lack of concern. Nat lies to his wife in order not to upset her. His wife displays a similar reaction when, after discovering the dead postman, she says: "I don't want Jill to see" (**34** 2).
- "Good old navy, they never let us down" (**34** 21).

The Englishman's pride in the navy is revealed in Nat's words. But his hopes are quickly dashed: what he has taken for the navy turns out to be a gigantic, rising and roaring mass of gulls.
- "The hawks ignored the windows" (**35** 20).

This fact is bound to cause the greatest anguish, because the birds of prey now concentrate their attack on the door and will most likely break through.
- "I'll smoke this last cigarette" (**35** 27).

Does this only mean the last cigarette of the packet, or Nat's last cigarette before the destruction of humanity?

## 2. For further discussion

*1. What possible explanations are given for the behaviour of the birds?*
- the birds' natural restlessness before the approach of winter (**11** 13–22)
- the change of weather (**14** 21–23)
- a "madness" (**14** 19)
- the Arctic Circle (**15** 21)
- the Russians have poisoned them (**21** 33)
- "some law the birds obeyed, ... to do with the east wind and the tide" (**26** 17–18)

- "an instinct to destroy mankind" (**35** 25)
*Give your own theory and explain it.*

*2. Why do you think Daphne du Maurier chose birds instead of insects or domestic animals?*

*3. How does the intensity of the birds' attacks increase in the course of the story?*
unidentified small birds—gulls—birds of prey tapping at the windowpanes—through the window in the children's bedroom—hammering at the door—down the chimney—splintering wood!

*4. Why is the story set in the country near the sea and not in the city?*

*5. How is the sense of the human being's isolation in the face of the forces of nature emphasized by the author?*

*6. Once you have read the whole story, comment on* **11** *24–26.*

*7. If Hitchcock's film is available, compare film and story.*

*8. Discuss whether the story has an open ending.*

Robley Wilson, Jr

# A Stay at the Ocean

On the sixth day of his vacation in the old house on Perkins Point, Stephen Bell woke, as usual, at five-thirty. The sun was on the wall opposite the small window of the bedroom, though the room was still chilly. Birds in the meadow behind the house made unintelligible conversation, and the remoteness of the ocean's noise suggested that the tide was out.

He got up and dressed. His wife, Clarice, was snoring becomingly in the big bed, and he paused on his way to the kitchen long enough to look into his daughter Linda's room and see her curly blond hair nestled into the corner of one elbow. He felt a strong possessiveness toward both his women, and a kindness; he did not wake them.

In the kitchen he quietly poured himself a glass of orange juice, washed a vitamin pill down with it, then set out on his customary walk to the sea.

The summer place, a modest white building the Bells had rented through an agent in Damariscotta, had been built in the twenties nearly at the tip of the point. From its upper windows it provided a view of the Atlantic in three directions, and while the point had very little sandy beach—only a strip of some hundred feet along the southwest edge—it had nearly three-quarters of a mile of shoreline along which Stephen could stroll in the early light. Rocks and split black ledges met the thrust of the sea with a kind of stubbornness, and brief reaches of lowland were strewn with coarse stones the ocean was rounding into its own toys. At the tip of the Point was something fairly worth calling a cliff; at high tide it dropped off five or six feet to the water; at low tide it became nearly impressive.

It was to the edge of this overhang that Stephen walked each day, to look at the sea and to assemble his private thoughts—this morning

---

4 **chilly** cool – 5 **remoteness** *here:* great distance from the listener – 7 **to snore** *schnarchen* – **becomingly** attractively – 13 **customary** [ˈkʌstəmərɪ] habitual – **Damariscotta** town near the coast of Maine; the story is set on the coast of Maine – 21 **ledge** narrow, flat place on the side of a cliff – 22 **thrust** sudden, forceful movement – **stubbornness** unwillingness to change one's mind – 23 **coarse** rough

## 38  Robley Wilson, Jr, A Stay at the Ocean

no different from any other. He noticed that the tide was remarkably low. Rocks he had never seen before had risen up off the end of the Point; his cliff plunged down not to green water, but to an unfamiliar shelf of darker stone which sloped gradually toward open sea. This morning the nearest tidal pool was so far away that it took all his strength to throw a stone hard enough to reach and ripple the smooth surface. Thrumcap Island, nearly a mile out, was an unaccustomed high shadow in the morning fog, and a few yards out from the tiny beach the blue rowboat which had come with the house sat aground on damp sand; the rope from its bow looked ridiculous, as if the boat were anchored somewhere under the earth.

"What's going on?" Stephen said, half to himself, but loud enough to startle a single gull overhead. The gull, which had appeared out of the fog, glided back into it. Stephen threw a last rock after it and returned to the house.

He found Clarice getting breakfast; Linda, in pajamas, had just poured a bowl of dry cereal and was now spilling a pitcher of milk over and around it.

"Did you get your pill?" Clarice asked.

"First thing." Stephen sat at the table across from his daughter. "You ought to see how low the tide is."

"The moon's full," his wife said. "It was low yesterday."

"I know, but this is *really* low. I've never seen anything like it."

Clarice set a plate of eggs before him. "Coffee's coming," she said. "Lin, please honey, eat over the bowl."

"You could walk halfway to Thrumcap," Stephen said.

Linda looked up from her cereal.

"No kidding, Lin. Halfway to Thrumcap."

"What do you suppose it is?" his wife said.

"Don't know," his mouth full. "What you said, I guess. The moon."

"Daddy, does the moon make tides?"

"So they say. Clarice? It's so low I can't throw a rock to the nearest water. And the boat's high and dry."

"How does the moon make tides?" Linda persisted.

---

3 **to plunge** [plʌndʒ] to dive – **unfamiliar** unknown – 4 **to slope** to become gradually lower from one end to the other – 7 **unaccustomed** unusual – 10 **bow** [baʊ] front part of a ship – 13 **to startle** to surprise and frighten slightly – **gull** *Möwe* – 17 **bowl** [boʊl] – **pitcher** *(AE)* jug *(BE) Krug* – 34 **to persist** to keep doing s.th. with determination

## Robley Wilson, Jr, A Stay at the Ocean

"Gravity," Stephen said. He winked at his daughter. "But you know what I think? I think this tide is too low for the moon to take credit for. I think the ocean is just a gigantic swimming pool, and somebody's draining it."

"Mother, *is* the ocean a big pool?"

"I think your father's teasing you." Clarice poured two cups of coffee and brought them to the table.

"*You* swim in it, don't you?" Stephen said.

"Everybody does."

"There you are. It's a pool, and somebody's draining it, and now we can walk halfway to Thrumcap."

Clarice frowned at him. "Drink your coffee, and stop feeding misinformation to eight-year-olds," she said.

Stephen patted his mouth with a napkin and pushed his chair back. "You think I'm making it all up," he said. "You come on and I'll show you."

By the time Stephen had jogged to the Point, the two women trailing after him, the fog had begun to burn away and Thrumcap Island stood monumentally ahead of them. The sea had receded still further; now over the mile between the Point and the island only a few round pools of water were left. All else was a waste of gray sand and flattened black weed. The island looked as if it had been lifted onto a plateau of sand, rimmed with twisted tree-roots.

Clarice stopped short. "Oh, Steve," she said. "Oh, Steve; my Lord."

"Is that something?" Stephen felt oddly as if he were taking credit for the phenomenon.

"Look at all the lobster traps!" Linda shouted.

Stephen looked. Where his daughter was pointing he saw a line of a dozen or so lobster pots mired in the channel about fifty yards out from the old shoreline. He started down the slope to the small beach.

"Let's have some lobsters," he called back.

"Steve, no. They belong to Paul Dunham."

He faced his wife. "But they'll just die, won't they? They won't be any good to anybody."

---

1 **gravity** *Schwerkraft* – 2 **to take credit for** to be responsible for – 4 **to drain** to let the water out – 6 **to tease** [ti:z] to make fun of s.o. gently – 12 **to frown** [fraʊn] to draw one's eyebrows together – 19 **to recede** [rɪˈsiːd] to move back – 22 **weed** wild plant, *here:* seaweed – 23 **rimmed with** having s.th. around the edge – 27 **lobster traps** *Hummerfallen* – 29 **to be mired** to be covered with mud

"Paul will get them."

"How? You can't run a boat through the sand."

"Then he'll walk. Stop showing your criminal side."

Stephen shrugged and came back.

"Aren't we going to have lobsters?" Linda said.

"We'll buy some, honey," Clarice told her. "Steve? Isn't this awfully strange?"

"I'll go along with that."

"I mean, this couldn't happen, could it? Are we just all having a dream?"

"You want me to pinch you?"

"Be serious, Steve." She sounded ready to cry.

He hugged her lightly. "I don't know, Clar. Yes, it's strange. It's impossible."

"Is it bad when the water goes so far away?" asked his daughter.

"No, Lin, it's just very funny. Very unusual and crazy." He looked at Clarice. "What do you want to do?"

"I don't know."

"Hey, I do. Let's all walk out to Thrumcap and explore. We've never done that before."

Linda danced. "Yes, let's."

"What if the tide comes back in?" Clarice said.

"Then we'll be marooned on the island and we'll hail a passing lobster boat."

"But if this is low tide—" Clarice hesitated. "What will high tide be like?"

"Slow. And we'll see it coming and run back to the house before it gets us." Stephen started down the beach. "Come on," he yelled, and his family followed after.

It was something like walking the edge of a usual beach, the sand packed hard, and the footprints of the three of them spreading into patterns of dryness as they walked. Except that there seemed no end to the beach. The sand was remarkably clean, Stephen noticed, with only random patches of seaweed beginning to dry in the sun, and here and there a mussel shell or a black crab half-buried. The sensation of

---

4 **to shrug** to raise one's shoulders – 11 **to pinch** to press s.th. (s.o.'s skin) between thumb and forefinger – 23 **to be marooned** to be unable to leave – 32 **patterns** arrangement of lines and shapes – 34 **random** without a plan or pattern – 35 **mussel** ['mʌsl] *Miesmuschel* – **crab** *Krabbe, Krebs*

actually walking to Thrumcap Island was eerie. He had never landed on Thrumcap—not even by boat. When they reached the island, he had to climb up to it, hand over hand, along and through the exposed roots of a tall pine, then reach down to pull Linda and Clarice ashore with him.

"It would be lovely to build a cottage out here, and just be isolated from everybody," Clarice said as they crossed the island.

"Would have been," Stephen agreed.

"Why say it that way?"

"I think the tide won't come back in. I think the ocean must be drying up, or changing its basin, or something."

"Are you serious?"

"I don't know. It doesn't make sense that this is just some fantastically low tide." They were standing now on the far side of the island, facing southeast. "Just look," he pointed out. "You can't even *see* the ocean."

He felt his wife's hand find his and squeeze hard. "I'm scared, Steve."

He put his other hand over hers. "Freak of nature," he said. "Let's walk back and see what's on the radio."

By the time they had started across to the Point, other figures were moving out from the old shore—men and women, and a few children; some of them were carrying picnic hampers. Dogs pranced around family groups or clawed and nosed at objects half-submerged in the sand. Not far from his own beach Stephen saw a lone man plodding toward a lobster trap, pulling a high-sided wooden child's wagon behind him.

"There's Paul," Clarice said. "Why don't you see what he knows about this? I'll take Lin up to the house and try to get some news."

They separated. Stephen caught up with the lobsterman. "Morning, Paul."

Dunham nodded to him. "Morning, Mr. Bell." He was a thin, fortyish man, needed a shave, had watery-gray eyes that looked out under a long-billed yachting cap. He had pulled on hip boots over his clothes; in the wagon Stephen could see a few lobsters moving sluggishly against each other. "What's happening, Paul?"

---

1 **eerie** strange and frightening, weird – 3 **exposed** not hidden; above the surface
19 **freak** *here:* unpredictable event – 23 **hamper** large basket with a lid – 34 **long-billed** *here:* with a long shade – **yachting** ['jɒtiŋ] – **hip** *Hüfte* – 35 **sluggishly** very slowly

"Can't say." He had come to the next of his string of traps, and had stooped to open it, drawing out a single lobster. He measured its carapace, then turned a perplexed look toward Stephen. "Don't know what to do with the damned thing," Dunham said. "Too small, but there's no place to throw the critter back to." He replaced the lobster in the trap and stood up.

"What's happened to the tide?" Stephen repeated.

Dunham gazed eastward. "Man up the coast told me it's gone out close to fifteen mile," he said. "Lives up on Pine Ledges. Owns a telescope."

"Will it come back in?"

Dunham picked up the the handle of the wagon. "I got my waders on," he said.

Stephen made an awkward gesture of parting. "Happy fishing," he said, stupidly.

He met his women near the beached rowboat. "Anything?" he asked.

"There's nothing on the radio but bad music," Clarice told him. "We should have brought the little TV with us. What do you want to do?"

"Look what some people are doing, Daddy."

"Steve, they're driving cars out there," Clarice exclaimed.

It was true. Stephen could see a half-dozen automobiles moving out toward Thrumcap, and the Schumanns—whose cottage was a few hundred yards northeast of theirs—had actually piled into their truck-camper and had just now driven off the beach, threading between two grounded sailboats toward the east.

"Let's do that," Stephen said.

"Drive out *there?*"

"Why not? Obviously it can support the weight."

"It would be fun," Linda said.

"Of course it would. Let's pack a lunch and get into the car and go."

"But go where?" Clarice wanted to know.

"To the ocean," Linda said.

"Right. That's what this vacation is all about. We'll drive to the ocean."

Clarice finally agreed, and in an hour the Bell car, a white compact station wagon, was packed for the outing. Clarice had made sand-

---

2 **to stoop** to bend over – **carapace** ['kærəpeɪs] shell of a lobster – 5 **critter** *(slang)* creature – 12 **waders** hip boots – 25 **to thread** [θred] *here:* to move in curves between objects – 37 **station wagon** *Kombi*

wiches and filled a Thermos with coffee. Stephen had put in a six-pack of beer, along with some hamburger and a carton of milk—all of it packed with ice in the metal chest. Linda had gathered together a careful selection of comic books and dolls. Almost as an afterthought, Stephen loaded the Coleman stove, and a five-gallon can of gasoline he had bought the day before for the outboard motor—explaining to his wife how unlikely it was they would be able to find either firewood or a gas station on the ocean floor.

"All set?" They were in the car, Linda curled in the back on a thin plaid mattress.

"All set," the women chorused.

Stephen was pleased that everything was turning out so well—that what might in some families have become a fearful time, a kind of domestic disaster in the face of the unexpected, was now resolved into one more vacation side-trip. Even Clarice seemed relaxed, though commonplace misgivings still plagued her.

"Do we have enough gas in the tank?"

"I filled it yesterday," he reassured her. "Cruising range: up to 500 miles."

"I hope nothing breaks down."

"Not a chance," Stephen said.

"Well," said his wife reluctantly, "just don't drive too fast."

It was easy to disobey her, Stephen discovered. The surface he drove on was unbelievably smooth, and though he once in a while was obliged to go around upjutting rocks or to avoid genuine islands that rose ahead of the car, the experience was very much like that of crossing a shopping-center parking lot—every destination reached by the straight-line distance, with no attention paid to lines painted by developers or highway commissioners. And the ride itself was luxurious: no bumps, no curves to speak of, the tires against the gray sand making a sound like skis on dry snow. The further he drove, the fewer the obstacles became; even with the speedometer needle swaying between 70 and 75, Clarice made no protest.

---

5 **Coleman stove** portable stove – 9 **to curl** [kɜːl] *here: sich zusammenrollen* – 10 **plaid** [plæd] *Schottenmuster* – 13 **domestic** in the home – 16 **misgivings** worry, doubts – 18 **to reassure** to take away worry – **cruising range** the distance it is possible to travel – 22 **reluctantly** unwillingly – 28 **developers** people or companies who buy land in order to build on it – 29 **highway commissioners** officials responsible for the highways – 30 **bump** *here:* uneven part of the road – 32 **obstacles** ['---] things that get in the way

Several cars passed him—none of them closer than ten yards—and the occupants of each car waved joyously and called out to the Bells.

"It's certainly a free-for-all," Clarice remarked.

"They're excited," Stephen said. "Nobody ever did *this* before."

"You couldn't even do this on television!" Linda shouted.

At the end of an hour-and-a-half of driving, Stephen was surprised to see a great number of cars—thirty or forty, he guessed—lined up about a mile ahead. They were stopped; the people in them had gotten out and were milling around.

"What's that all about?" Clarice asked.

"Maybe the road's washed out," Stephen suggested. He winked at his wife.

"You're so damned funny," she said.

"I bet it's the ocean," Linda said.

"Hey, I'll bet you're right." He slowed down and eased the wagon to a stop between two of the parked cars. "Okay," he said, "everybody out."

But it wasn't the ocean. Walking in front of the car, the three of them found themselves at the edge of a steep bluff.

"Wow!" said Linda. "Look how far down it is."

It was more than 200 feet to the bottom of the bluff—not a perpendicular drop, but a perilously steep angle from where they stood down to what appeared to be a limitless dry plain. The cliff consisted primarily of coarse rock, partly bare, partly encrusted with green and white shell-things. Deep crevices between the outcroppings of stone were filled with sand. The plain below seemed entirely of sand, and looked flat as a table top.

"We'll never get down there," Stephen said. He heard a touch of awe in his own voice.

"Quite a sight, isn't it?"

The words startled him; he turned and found himself facing a stranger—a middle-aged man with rusty hair and plump chins.

"Incredible," Stephen agreed.

"There's a couple of guys down the line say they're going to try and drive a Jeep down to the valley. I say they're batty."

---

9 **to mill around** to move around in a disorganized way – 19 **bluff** cliff – 21 **perpendicular** ['dɪk] vertical *(senkrecht)* – 22 **perilously** dangerously – 25 **crevice** large, narrow crack in a rock – 29 **awe** feeling of respect and amazement – 32 **rusty** *here:* colour of rust – **plump** rather fat – 35 **batty** slightly mad

Stephen nodded soberly. "I should think so."

"Me and the wife, we're going to head south from here."

"Why south?" Clarice was asking the question.

The stranger hesitated and put out his hand. "Excuse me, folks," he said. "The name's Allen. We're out here from Des Moines."

Introductions were exchanged. Mrs Allen, a dowdy facsimile of her husband, joined them.

"We met this gentleman from New York," Allen told them, "says he used to study geology in college. He claims that if you drive a couple of hundred miles south—down near Cape Cod, he says—and then head straight east, you won't have to run up against this particular cliff. I don't know, but he claims he does."

"That's interesting," Clarice said.

"Says you can drive right out on this Continental Shelf he used to study about," Allen added.

Stephen looked at his wife. "Want to try it?"

"Are you and Mrs Allen going to do that?" Clarice asked.

"Oh yes; we surely are."

"What for?"

"Curiosity, mostly," Allen told her. He seemed reluctant to say more.

"And the treasure," Mrs Allen put in.

"Treasure?" Linda was suddenly interested.

"Oh, well, yes, we sort of thought we'd look around for a little sunken treasure." Allen shuffled uneasily as he spoke. "You know, all those old ships that went down—oh, hundreds of years ago—and up to now nobody's been able to find 'em. We thought we'd keep an eye out. You saw that old hulk on the way here?"

"No, we didn't," Stephen said.

"Oh, we drove past it. Half-buried thing. No way to get inside it."

"But we've got shovels in the pickup," Mrs Allen said.

Allen began drifting away with his wife. "We'd better get started," he told Stephen. "Have a safe trip."

"Steve? Does that make sense? Finding sunken treasure?"

He gave a small, noncommittal gesture with his arms. "At this point, I'll believe anything. How about eating? It's way past noon."

---

1 **soberly** in a serious manner – 5 **Des Moines** capital of the State of Iowa – 6 **dowdy** [ˈdaʊdɪ] shabby, untidy – **facsimile** [fækˈsɪmɪlɪ] exact copy – 24 **to shuffle** to move one's feet about while standing – 27 **hulk** *here:* body of a ship – 30 **shovel** [ˈʃʌvl] *Schaufel* – **pickup** small truck with an open back – 34 **noncommittal** not willing to say exactly what one thinks

### 46  Robley Wilson, Jr, A Stay at the Ocean

"But we haven't seen any old hulks," Clarice said.

"True, but it stands to reason there must *be* some. There ought to be a lot of Second World War shipping scattered around somewhere, too."

"We haven't seen anything. Not even any dead fish, or those strange underwater plants you see pictures of. Why is that?"

He passed around sandwiches. "I suppose everything got buried under silt or swept out clean. This was some tide, you know."

They ate. Stephen sat on the fender of the car, the sandwich in one hand, a beer in the other. As he gazed out over the edge of the bluff he marveled at how far he could see, and how little was to be seen. The horizon—How far away? Twenty? Thirty miles?—was as unbroken as the rim of a plate. God knew where the ocean was, what it was doing, how long it would recede from them. He shook his head, as if to wake himself up. Off to his right, a young couple in white deck-shoes was gingerly climbing over the edge of the cliff. He leaned forward to get a glimpse of the precipitous slope. The couple was picking black, withered plants out of a thin river of sand. They climbed back up, obviously delighted with what they had done. Off to his left, a small boy was sailing bottlecaps far out and down to the plain; the caps glided like odd birds. Where were the gulls and cormorants? he suddenly wondered. Following the elusive sea?

"Let's take that drive south," he said to his wife.

"Should we, Steve?"

"We won't get lost. I'll move in so we can see the shore on the way down."

"We ought to go back to the house first, don't you think? Maybe we should get the tent, and some more food."

"No," he said, "let's be really adventurous. There's food enough for breakfast, and we can sleep in the car if we have to."

It occurred to him as he backed the car around and set a course for the southwest that he had to go as far as he could—as if something in him insisted that he find the ocean. He rationalized the insistence in two ways: first, the ocean was what he had left Cleveland for, and he

---

2 **it stands to reason** it is obvious – 8 **silt** fine sand, soil or mud – 9 **fender** *(AE)* mudguard *(BE) Kotflügel* – 11 **to marvel** to be filled with surprise – 16 **gingerly** ['dʒɪndʒəlɪ] with great caution – 17 **precipitous** [prɪ'sɪpɪtəs] high and steep – **to wither** to dry out (plants) – 22 **elusive** [ɪ'lu:sɪv] difficult to find or grasp – 33 **to rationalize** to think of ways to explain s.th. – 34 **Cleveland** city in Ohio, on Lake Erie

## Robley Wilson, Jr, A Stay at the Ocean 47

refused to be deprived of it after fifty weeks of slaving over his drafting board; second, he certainly wanted to be able to tell his friends, firsthand, what that Great Tide business had been all about. *I was there,* he could say. *I was part of it.*

"Now there's land in front of us," Clarice was saying.

He had been driving for two hours since lunch, making good time as before, except that there had been considerable cross-traffic to keep him alert—cars, campers, motorcycles, all moving madly east. He had kept the New England coast in sight most of the way—*the old coast.*

"Let's go ashore and see where we are," he said.

What he had in mind was to stretch his legs in some kind of normal place, to find restrooms and buy gas, to keep his ears open for any news sifted in from the larger world. The landfall turned out to be the Gloucester peninsula, and Stephen was able to drive up out of the ocean bottom across a pebbled beach not far from a paved highway. In the nearest town he pulled into a gas station. Reading a road map while a sullen young man filled his tank, Stephen concluded that the town was Rockport, and he tried to estimate—referring to a sun that was by now halfway down the sky—which direction to set out in to avoid driving into Cape Cod Bay.

In twenty minutes they were on their way southeast; the attendant had refused to honor his credit card—another driver at the station had complained loudly—and Stephen had paid what seemed an unusually high price for the gas. *Frightened,* Stephen decided; *taking the cash while he can.*

He drove casually and fast; he was getting used to this sort of travel, to the experience of other cars strewn as far as the eye could see in every direction.

"It's something like an old-fashioned land rush," he said to Clarice.

"I suppose," she said. "Did you hear any news at the gas station?"

"Rumors, is all."

"Well, like what?"

He pursed his lips. "Silly things. Some guy told me he'd heard most of Europe was under water."

---

1 **to be deprived of** to have to do without s.th. unwillingly – **drafting board** *Zeichenbrett* – 8 **to be alert** to pay full attention to what is happening – 12 **restroom** *(AE)* toilet – 13 **landfall** the first bit of land seen after a voyage at sea – 15 **pebbled** covered in smooth round stones – 17 **sullen** bad-tempered – 26 **casually** in a relaxed way – 29 **land rush** cf Gold Rush – 31 **rumor** a possibly untrue story that is passed on – 33 **to purse one's lips** to draw one's lips together into a small, rounded shape

*48 Robley Wilson, Jr, A Stay at the Ocean*

"My God, Steve."
"Oh, come on, Clar. That's hardly likely, you know."
"I *don't* know." She slouched into the corner by the door. "The water must have gone somewhere."
"Believe anything you want. Maybe it's Judgment Day."
His wife kept quiet.
Of course it was possible—that wild story about Europe. It was strangely logical, Stephen admitted. Still, fantastic. How could you explain it? A shift in the magnetic poles, maybe. Or a meteor—something huge—hitting the earth with incredible force. But wouldn't there have been earthquakes? He mused, scarely thinking about his driving—not needing to. There were no obstructions, nothing to slow down for.
"I can't say much for the scenery," he said.
"Daddy, my stomach hurts," Linda complained.
He glanced at his watch. It was after six o'clock, he was amazed to notice; he had lost track of time since leaving Rockport, and surely his daughter had a right to be hungry.
"Be patient, honey," Clarice said in a tone part soothing, part mocking. "Daddy will stop as soon as he finds a nice shady spot."
He smirked. "Now *that's* funny," he said, yet almost at once he was startled to see something black on the horizon. He pointed. "What do you suppose that is?"
"I don't know," Clarice said, "but let's stop there."
Closer, he identified the object.
"There's our first shipwreck," he said. It looked, as he drew toward it, to be a modern ship—metal-hulled, at any rate—stern up as if it had dived sharply to the bottom. Second World War? Victim of a submarine? Its enormous square plates were deep red with rust, and its unexpected presence made the miles of sand around it all the more desolate. Circling to the ship's shady side he saw that two other cars were already parked alongside it.
"Company," he said.
"That's good," Clarice decided. "You'll have somebody to talk to while I get supper."

---

3 **to slouch** [slaʊtʃ] to hang or lean downwards – 5 **Judgement Day** the day when God will judge everyone (Christian tradition) – 19 **to soothe** [suːð] to make someone feel calmer – **to mock** to make fun of s.o. – 21 **to smirk** [smɜːk] to smile in an unpleasant way – 27 **metal-hulled** with a metal hull, i.e. body – 33 **company** *here:* people to talk to

Stephen parked and got out. People from one of the cars spread a cloth under the lengthening shadow of the hulk. A man appeared on top of the wreck and peered down over the crusted railing, hanging on to keep his balance against the rake of the deck.

"Looking for the ocean?" he called down to Stephen.

"It's all in here." He pointed toward the submerged bow. Leaving the women to fix the hamburgers, Stephen walked around the ship and made his way precariously up the steep deck. "I think it must have been a tanker," the man above him said.

"Torpedoed?"

"I expect so." The man wore Bermudas and a Hawaiian shirt; he grinned at Stephen. "Makes you feel like Davy Jones, doesn't it? I looked into that hatch down there. Couldn't see anything, but I could hear water sloshing. Bet there's a lot of bones rolling around in there; poor bastards."

Stephen nodded. He didn't feel like talking, but stayed on the ship, bracing himself against a ventilator. To be above the ocean's floor was pleasant; the air was warm and windless; he even enjoyed the difficulty of keeping his balance, after hours of cramped driving.

Certainly this had been the most remarkable day of his life—of all their lives—and filled with small wonders. The lobsterman pulling his coaster wagon. The foolish couple from Iowa with their shovels and dreams of treasure. The boy and girl at the cliff, acting like honemooners picking edelweiss in the Alps. And the ocean. The ocean he had grown used to in summer after summer of holidays in Maine—suddenly turned into a desert. Still—He felt a faint shiver of apprehension. If there was water in the hold of this broken tanker—

He edged his way to the open hatch, a gaping black hole in the rust and scale of the deck-plates, and tried to see inside. It smelled like ocean, he thought. He listened, and could hear the water. *Why should it be moving?* Stephen stepped off the hulk and looked around. Nothing—but was that fog, far off to the east?

---

3 **to peer** to look very hard – **crusted** covered with a hard, uneven substance – 4 **rake** sloping position – 8 **precariously** [prɪˈkeərɪəslɪ] with very insecure movements – 12 **Davy Jones** evil spirit of the sea; sailors' devil – 13 **hatch** opening in the deck of a ship – 14 **to slosh** to sound like water moving back and forth – 15 **bastard** *(slang) here:* unfortunate person – 17 **to brace yourself against s.th.** to press against s.th. in order to avoid falling – 26 **faint** weak, slight – **shiver** trembling – **apprehension** a feeling of fear that s.th. terrible may happen – 29 **scale** thin pieces of rust, like the scales of a fish

50 *Robley Wilson, Jr, A Stay at the Ocean*

Stephen called up to the man in Bermudas. "Do you hear anything?"

"No," the man said. Stephen noticed a car, about a mile away, headed west. "Wait a minute," the man said. "I do hear something."

It was the sound he had awakened to that morning—of the tide, far far out.

"By George," the man said, "I think we've found her at last." He stumbled down from the deck. "We've caught up with her," he said, and went to tell his family.

Stephen walked back to the women.

"Not ready yet," Clarice said. "Why don't you open a can of beer?"

He took a deep breath. "Listen, I think we'd better start back. It's about a hundred-and-fifty miles to Cape, but we ought to be able to get there just after dark."

Clarice tensed. "What is it?" she said.

"I just think we'd better go. It's been a long day."

His wife turned off the stove and dumped the meat onto the sand. "Linda, get in the car."

"Don't we get to eat anything?"

"Linda, honey, don't quibble with me." She glanced around. The two neighboring cars were gone. Other cars appeared from the east and sped past.

"I'm going to put that spare gasoline in the tank," Stephen said, "just so we won't have to stop."

As he worked, he could hear the soft, incessant whisper of waves at his back. He made a botch of pouring the gas. *Steady,* he told himself. *It's your own damned fault.*

When he finished, the women were inside, waiting. He tossed the gasoline can away in a high, tumbling arc, and hurried to get into the car. The sea noise behind them was by now so loud that he could hear it even above the engine as it burst into life. He shifted into first gear and skidded forward.

"Tides come in gradually, don't they?" Clarice said in a tight voice.

---

7 **by George** euphemism for "by God" – 13 **Cape** Cape Code – 15 **to tense** to feel oneself stiffen out of fear – 20 **to quibble** to argue about small, unimportant matters – 25 **incessant** [ın'sesnt] without stopping – 26 **to make a botch of s.th.** to do s.th. badly – 29 **to tumble** to fall with a rolling movement – **arc** curve – 32 **to skid** to slide sideways

*Robley Wilson, Jr, A Stay at the Ocean* 51

"Usually," Stephen said. He threw the shift lever into second; again the rear wheels of the station wagon spun, as if the sand under them were getting wetter.

"I just can't believe any of this," his wife said. She leaned her head against the back of the seat and closed her eyes.

Now he was in high gear. The engine was turning over smoothly and the speedometer needle stood unwaveringly at seventy miles an hour. Ahead of him the evening sun was sliding down to the horizon; he kept the car headed toward it, squinting across the enormous reach of gray sand. *What a queer thing,* he thought. *What a devil of a way to finish a vacation.* He was aware all around him of other cars, other drivers, all racing west on this incredible aimless track. One car passed him, then another, and he pushed the accelerator down. He overtook a white camper and swerved around it; the station wagon fishtailed slightly.

"What's the matter?" His wife opened her eyes.

"Nothing's the matter."

"We won't run out of gas now, will we?"

"Not a chance." He watched the needle slide past eighty. The sand was glistening ahead of him, water seeping to the surface. The tide must be racing in behind them. Could they swim free? Where would they swim to?

"Daddy!" The scream startled him. "Daddy, I can see it! I can see it coming after us!" Linda wasn't crying. In the rearview mirrow he could see her face, half-turned in his direction, her eyes vivid, her mouth working desperately to make more words. Out the back window he could make out a low gray wall that seemed to be gaining on him. Under his wheels he could hear water splashing, see spray flying. He switched on the wipers.

He reached over and squeezed his wife's hand. *At least we're all together,* he thought. Off to the right he saw an overturned car, two men and a woman out trying to turn it upright. The sun was almost at the horizon and its light cast back a hundred rainbows through the wakes of a hundred cars. A pale, pebbly mist began forming on surfaces in-

---

1 **shift lever**['li:və] *Hebel der Gangschaltung* – 2 **to spin** (spun, spun) to turn quickly – 9 **to squint** to look with your eyes partly closed – 10 **queer** strange, odd – 14 **to fishtail** to move from side to side – 20 **to glisten** to shine, to sparkle – **to seep** to flow slowly through – 25 **vivid** very bright – 26 **desperately** in panic – 27 **to gain on** to catch up with – 29 **wipers** *Scheibenwischer* – 33 **wakes** *here:* tracks the cars leave behind them

side the car. The roar of the impossible tide was deafening; it seemed now to be all around him, and the deepening water drummed like hammers against the metal under the car. He was thinking irrelevantly of how quickly the salt sea would rust out the fenders and rocker panels when he heard Clarice for the last time, shrieking:

"Drive, Steve, drive. For pity's sake, drive, drive, *drive!*"

4 **rocker panels** *(AE)* shock absorbers *(Stoßdämpfer)*

**Biographical Notes**

*ROBLEY WILSON, Jr (1930– ) was born in Maine. He has been a professor of English and Russian at several American universities. His writings include fiction, poetry and critical essays. Many of his stories and poems have been published in literary journals and popular magazines.*

# Summary and Teaching Notes

## Summary

Stephen Bell, his wife Clarice and their daughter Linda are spending their vacation on the coast of Maine, facing the Atlantic Ocean.
Very early one morning Steve walks to the beach and discovers that an exceptionally low tide has exposed rocks that are normally submerged, leaving boats and an island high and dry. When he returns to the house, his family at first express a certain disbelief. They all go down to the beach, where they walk around in mild amazement, climb onto the island, meet other excited people and learn from a lobster-pot owner that the tide may well be fifteen miles out. Noticing that people are driving their cars out eastwards, Steve decides to follow suit. He and his family load up their station wagon and drive on the barren ocean bed, heading east. Other cars overtake them, full of people in high spirits. After driving for an hour and a half they reach the edge of the Continental Shelf, a two-hundred-foot cliff. Even here there is no sign of the ocean. They meet various people with whom they chat and discuss this freak event. It is then that Steve decides to drive further south, spurred on by a spirit of adventure and a secret desire to boast about it later. After a while they come across an old war-time shipwreck. Examining the old hulk Steve feels a faint shiver of apprehension, as he perceives a fog far out to the east and hears the sound of the tide. Hastily Steve starts to drive back towards the mainland, 150 miles away.
From then on events move swiftly. Steve drives as fast as he can. Other cars race past in a headlong flight. Anxiety gives way to fear, then to panic. With a sort of calm anguish Steve realizes that the tide is catching up on them. The story ends with Clarice uttering a shriek of terror as the tide overwhelms them.

# Teaching Notes

## 1. The story in its parts

For the purposes of our interpretation we will divide the story into three parts.

### I  A vacation interrupted by an unexpected event (37 1–40 29)

*1. Describe the atmosphere at the beginning.*
The atmosphere is peaceful, suited to a vacation, as suggested by the title. Terms such as "as usual" (**37** 2) and "customary" (**37** 13) underline the normality of the situation. The mention of the sun, the birds, the family sleeping and Stephen's feelings ("a kindness" **37** 11) evoke positive emotions.

*2. What are the first signs that something unusual has occurred?*
– the exceptionally low tide
– rocks that Steve has never seen before
– the nearest tidal pool a stone's throw away
– Thrumcap Island "an unaccustomed high shadow" (**38** 7–8)
– the blue rowboat stuck on the sand
– Steve's question: "What's going on?" (**38** 12)
It is clear that Steve has no idea of what is going on; nor has the reader. The tone of mystery—puzzlement—is set. Nor shall we ever know what is going on!

*3. Describe the nature and the tone of the conversation when Steve returns.*
Steve and his family employ commonplace, routine speech, ready-made phrases and remarks, few long words. *Find examples.* The conversation alternates between everyday concerns (" 'Lin, please honey, eat over the bowl' " **38** 25) and the extraordinary phenomenon of the tide (" 'I've never seen anything like it' " **38** 23). This, and Stephen's teasing of his daughter, makes the tone light-hearted, though edged with uncertainty.

*4. How do the three members of the family react when they see the low tide?*
*Steve* is conceited, feeling "oddly as if he were taking credit for the phenomenon" (**39** 25–26) and irresponsible: " 'We'll see it coming and run back to the house before it gets us' " (**40** 27–28).
*Clarice* has a feeling of unease: " 'Oh, Steve; my Lord' " (**39** 24); " 'Isn't this awfully strange?' " (**40** 6–7); "She sounded ready to cry" (**40** 12); " 'What will high tide be like?' " (**40** 25–26). This contrasts with the seeming indifference she showed at the house, when she could not yet comprehend the situation.
*Linda* displays a child's curiosity and excitement: " 'Is it bad when the water goes so far away?' " (**40** 15); " 'Yes, let's' " (**40** 21).

*5. What is the effect of the contrast between familiar daily routine and the freak event?*
It is a common literary device to start a story with a calm, peaceful setting, where nothing much happens and ordinary people just wander around enjoying life or are busy with their work. Such a setting can lull readers into a sense of ease or even false security. A "freak" event bursting in is therefore all the more outstanding by contrast, as people will react more or less incoherently, excitedly, incredulously, stupidly even.
A "freak" event strikes the imagination more and affects the feelings most strongly if all around is, or appears, normal.

**II An adventurous outing** (**40** 30–**47** 25)

*1. How does the conversation on Thrumcap Island reveal Clarice's and Steve's personalities?*
Clarice's dream of an isolated cottage on the island shows her desire for happy solitude. She cannot take the freak event lightly ("I'm scared, Steve" **41** 17–18).
Steve's conviction that the tide won't come back (**41** 10–11) reveals the self-assurance that will later make him act in an irresponsible way.

*2. Steve decides to drive east. How do his wife and daughter feel about it?*

Clarice seems doubtful at first but finally gives in to her husband (**42** 35). Linda is excited, thinking it would be fun.

It may be helpful for students to visualize the car trip by progressively sketching a rough plan of the family's movements, starting with the drive east to the Continental Shelf, then tracing the drive southwards and west to the coast (Rockport), then south-east, as the family moves further from the coast to avoid driving into Cape Cod Bay. After leaving the hulk they head due west again.

*3. Which details indicate that the drive eastward on the ocean bed is viewed as a holiday adventure?*
– a picnic lunch, cans of beer, the starting call (" 'All set?' " **43** 9)
– the pleasant sensation of speed, the cheerfulness of other people driving past.

*4. What do we learn about Stephen from the sentence, "Stephen was pleased..." (***43** 12–15)?
This reflects Stephen's determination not to let his world—his very domestic world—be disturbed by the event. A common strategy for dealing with threat is to ignore it and pretend that life can go on as usual. Clarice's "misgivings" are only "commonplace" in Steve's eyes.

*5. How do various people behave once they reach the edge of the cliff?*
– The "batty" ones try to drive a jeep down.
– A young couple picks "flowers".
– A small boy makes bottle caps sail down.
– Others decide to drive south in order to avoid the Continental Shelf and to find hypothetical treasure.

All of this behaviour is bizarre under the circumstances—" 'You couldn't even do this on television!' " (Linda **44** 5).

Students could be asked about the effect of this behaviour on the reader: increasing the reader's sense of incredulity and heightening suspense as the reader wonders what could happen next.

*6. What details strike Steve and his family as being rather odd during their picnic lunch?*
– no dead fish, no plants, no birds
– excellent visibility, but practically nothing to be seen

There is no doubt that the strangeness of this unearthly, lifeless landscape contributes to a feeling of unease.

*7. What pushes Steve to drive on?*
He wants to find the ocean, the embodiment of his vacation (**42** 34, **46** 34–**47** 2).
He is spurred on by a spirit of adventure and wants to boast later about the "Great Tide" (**47** 2–4).

*8. Comment on Steve's judgement of the gas station attendant: "Frightened, taking the cash while he can" (**47** 24–25).*
The students should find out what actually happens at the filling station: the attendant refuses to accept credit cards and overcharges. He may be apprehensive that no more tourits will come if the ocean disappears, or he foresees that the credit cards will not be honoured later because the owners might be dead or lost. This adds to the sense of foreboding present already.

**III The adventure ends in a catastrophe** (**47** 26–end)

*1. How is the catastrophe foreshadowed?*
– wild rumours: Europe under water (**47** 33–34)
– " 'Maybe it's Judgment Day.' " (**48** 5)
– more or less implausible explanations of the phenomenon (**48** 8–11)
– the shipwreck as a symbol of disintegration, the presence of human bones in the shipwreck (**48** 26–**49** 15)
– the bareness of the area that evokes a sense of loneliness and desolation (**49** 24–26)

*2. Which sounds accompany the family's increasing nervousness and fear, as events move swiftly to their climax?*
– sound of water sloshing in the hatch
– sound of the tide far out
– the soft incessant whisper of waves, louder than the engine
– the increasing roar of the ocean behind them
– Linda's scream: " 'Daddy, I can see it!' "
– the deafening roar

- the water drumming like hammers
- Clarice's last shriek of despair

Note how in the last three paragraphs a lot of attention is paid to impressions of sight and sound. This places the reader in the middle of the situation, together with the family.

The phenomenon of a low tide causing the ocean to recede and even disappear is obviously an impossibility. We are therefore in a make-believe situation, but readers are willing and even eager to accept this as long as the characters in the story are realistic and genuine, as long as their reactions and general behaviour are plausible, as is the case in this story.

## 2. Characters

a) *Stephen* is the principal character. He is a natural type, young, dynamic, confident but also slightly superficial and boastful. He is ultimately responsible for the tragedy that befalls him and his family.

*Look at **42** 27 (" 'Let's do that,' Stephen said.") and **46** 23 (" 'Let's take that drive south' "). What do these two quotes reveal of Stephen's character?*

Stephen alone takes all the decisions, following other people's example, failing to consider possible consequences. He loses his sense of time, thus forgetting that the tide normally turns after six hours and that therefore it would have been wiser to return and not remain 150 miles from the mainland.

When he realizes that it is his "*own damned fault*"(**50** 27), it is too late, and his only consolation is: "*At least we're all together*" (**51** 30-31).

b) *Clarice* is reluctant to take the risks which she feels are connected with this adventure: She is afraid that they may run out of gas or have a breakdown, they may not have enough food, they may have to spend the night outdoors, and, above all, that the tide will come back. Despite her fears she gives in to her husband.

*What function do Clarice's misgivings fulfill for the reader?*
They mirror, or awaken, doubts in the reader.

c) *Linda* is a natural eight-year-old girl. She likes excitement, is keen on doing something out of the ordinary, likes adventure and treasure-hunting, but when she is hungry she forgets everything else. Her presence in the story adds a light-hearted note and emphasizes Steve's irresponsibility, since he is risking her life as well.

d) *Minor characters*
*Make a list of the minor characters in the story and discuss their various functions.*
– *Paul Dunham*, the taciturn lobster-catcher, provides a contrast to Stephen. Paul is not looking for adventure and thinks practically (" 'I got my waders on' " **42** 12–13).
– *Mr and Mrs Allen*, the rather comic couple from Des Moines, provide Stephen with the impulse to go even further. Together with the daring types planning to go down the cliff and the couple picking "flowers", they illustrate the desire to fulfill some kind of impossible dream in the extraordinary situation created by the tide.
– *The sullen attendant at the gas station*, who accepts cash only, increases the sense of foreboding.
– *The man at the hulk*, wearing Bermudas and a Hawaiian shirt, draws Stephen's attention to the presence of water.
All of these characters behave in a plausible manner. They are figures one could meet anytime. The incredible event takes place against a backdrop of normality.

## 3. Dialogues

The conversations are lively, light-hearted, even superficial, as befits a holiday mood.
In this story the author has used dialogue to a considerable extent. Discussions and conversations link events. (The students should find examples.) They inform us of how decisions are reached, and why. In fact each decision is preceded by a short discussion, usually of a light-hearted nature or held in a jesting manner. In this way an explanation of events and subsequent action is supplied. The final shriek of terror is in itself sufficient to make us understand what happens.

In the course of conversations attempts are made to offer explanations for the disappearance of the ocean, and how unreal it all seems. As it is ordinary people who try to give these explanations, these are bound to be wild, fanciful and improbable, the result of guess-work rather than of scientific knowledge and logical thinking.

## 4. For further discussion

*1. Discuss Steve's responsibility in the tragedy that befalls him and his family.*

*2. Do you think that despite the improbable nature of the main phenomenon—the disappearance of the ocean—a moral can be drawn from this story? Can such "disaster" stories serve a purpose?*

*3. Which aspects of the story seem to be particularly American?*
Students might point to features of dialogue (" 'please honey' "; " 'my Lord' "; " 'critters' "; " 'we surely are' "). The importance of the car in the story may also be considered typical for America. Steve and his family drive into their adventure, as do many others. One might also ask in what way Steve's vitamin pill is part of the cultural setting.

*4. Try to imagine other extraordinary ecological catastrophes like the one in the story "A Stay at the Ocean".* (The students could be asked to construct a plot, perhaps in small groups.)

Anonymous

# Jambawal the Thunder Man

The whites are coming back—pouring in from the sky by plane, by helicopter, even by parachute. Soon the whole mob will be back and even more eager than they were before. The machines will begin to roll, rattle and roar and the town will begin to rise again; it will grow again like a forest, but such an ugly forest of concrete and steel, growing out of heaps of junk and rubbish. No, there's no way to outwit the whites; but the night before last Jambawal—Cyclone the whites call him—had a pretty good try. One sweep this way and another there, and now in the whole town, there's hardly a tree or a pole left standing. I can't see a single building that isn't smashed or torn by Jambawal's visit.

I'm glad he made it at last. Since they brought me here to the island I've watched the sky and called to him. I knew he'd come someday. I knew if I called, and waited long enough, Jambawal would rise from Bralgu to sweep across the sea in such a rage that when he hit the town the white man and his houses would flutter like leaves in the air. Sometimes I climbed to the island peak, high, like an ant-hill there, and looking toward Bralgu I danced and sang to Jambawal—not so loud as to annoy him, but gently; just enough to remind him that he must come.

Perhaps I should have called to Jambawal more often, to make him come sooner—there's nothing left now to save from the whites. They have already cleaned the bush and bulldozed the black man's land. They have built their houses and made their graveyard—the country I knew well is ugly and strange. No black man now can point to a place and say: "Here, at the bottom of this waterhole (please don't disturb)

---

**Jambawal** ['---] ancestor-being (in the belief of the Aboriginal people of this story) who comes in storm clouds from the islands to the coast – 2 **mob** large, disorganized group of people with a common aim – 3 **eager** keen, highly motivated – 5 **concrete** *Beton* – 6 **junk** old or useless things – **to outwit s.o.** to gain an advantage over s.o. by being clever – 7 **cyclone** *Wirbelsturm* – 8 **sweep** wide, smooth movement – 9 **pole** straight length of wood or metal, standing upright – 12 **to make it** to arrive – 15 **Bralgu** land of the dead (in Aboriginal belief) and of the ancestor spirits – 17 **ant** *Ameise* – 26 **to disturb** to unsettle

## 54  Anon., Jambawal the Thunder Man

lies the spirit of our ancestor. That emu, see it, was once a black woman who burned her hands and became an earthbound bird. The Banyan tree—now, that was planted by Djanggawul to shelter our people from the hot sun." Even the trampled space where we danced to call for rain when drought was long—that has been taken by the white man.

It's not for myself that I am sorry Jambawal came late, but for young fellas like Tommy and Wonbri. If Jambawal had heard me sooner there may have been something of the black man's land left for the young ones—but here in gaol they don't give you much time to call on your ancestors and ask for help. In the old days the whites would chain you to a tree and leave you alone—you could stay there for days, for weeks may be, with no food and still be happy. The ancestors from the Dreaming will care for you if you're alone long enough to call on them—and when the ancestors hear, and come to you, you're never alone again. The whites have changed their ways, though and it's hard to call the Dreaming. Now they put a great sledge-hammer in your hands, and bully you to swing it against the rocks from dawn till dark. When night comes and you're pushed into the lock-up, you lie down without the strength to sigh or swear.

I should climb up to the top of the peak, now—the view from the highest rocks goes far beyond the town and I'd like to see what Jambawal has done to my country but no ... I'd better stay. Malug might wake from his strange sleep. He may need me; he might want to say something—to make a last wish or give me some advice before he's away to Bralgu for ever. Poor bloke, he's really been unlucky—or maybe not; maybe it's a good way to die, to pass on to Bralgu. I don't think Jambawal meant to hurt Malug though. He was after the white man and Malug got in the way; he wouldn't harm a blackfella. Even crows and dingoes won't hurt their own kind.

I wish Malug could talk. There's so much to say and no one about to answer. Jambawal struck late at night—the best time to surprise the white man, to knock down his house, to scatter him frightened and half asleep with a Bible in one hand and a gun in the other. Jambawal

---

1 **emu** ['iːmjuː] large, flightless Australian bird  – 3 **Banyan tree** tropical kind of fig tree *(ficus)* – **Djanggawul** Creator who gave birth to the people and gave spirit to animals and plants – 4 **to trample** to tread on many times – 5 **drought** [draʊt] long period without rain – 10 **gaol** [dʒeɪl] – 14 **Dreaming** world of origins, source of creation and sacred power – 17 **sledge-hammer** large, heavy hammer – 18 **to bully** ['bʊlɪ] to force s.o. to do s.th. – 23 **Malug** person's name – 26 **bloke** *(slang)* man – 30 **crow** Krähe – **dingo** wild Australian dog – 33 **to scatter** to send in all different directions

*Anon., Jambawal the Thunder Man* 55

must have been really angry. I have never before heard his voice so loud or felt the earth tremble and quiver like a beaten snake. He seemed to be trying to blow the sea from its bed, to roll it over the town and the white men. The roof of the gaol flew away, and the walls slid down around us like a rotten fence. It was a pity the guards had gone—I would have liked to see them frightened and angry, but powerless to punish the wind. They were lucky that Jambawal came in the night, for they're never here after dark. As soon as they've locked the doors behind the five of us, away they go—rushing to the boat which will carry them across the bay to their own mob.

Did Malug say something then? It sounded as though he called—but no, I must have dreamed it. He hasn't spoken; didn't even yell for help when we called and searched for him. When the wind was high we thought he had blown away to the sea, and when dawn came we searched the rocks and the beach. But much later Tommy saw a hand, with clutching fingers, reaching from the wreck of the gaol. Perhaps Jambawal meant to carry Malug clear away to Bralgu and knocked the gaol in his hurry, for a whole wall of concrete and stone lay on top of him, and the rest of the building scattered all about.

It looks as if Mopoke had better luck. A big, tall, blackfella he was, with tribal marks on his chest and only a few words of the white man's talk. The police brought him in a few days ago, maybe from somewhere deep in the bush—I couldn't understand his tribal lingo but we called him Mopoke. He sat up at night, not sleeping, and maybe he called Jambawal to take him back to the bush or to the Dreaming. Looks like he made it, too. We found his shorts, this morning, on the beach, washed up by the sea. He must have sent them back from Bralgu—you don't need the white man's rags there.

Malug's moving his lips. I cleared the rocks from around his head and he seems to be able to move a little. Perhaps he's trying to speak ... no, it's water he wants, and there's not a drop. I can pretend to be looking about for some, I suppose, but the water-tank blew off its stand with the first wind and all the taps are dry. If Tommy and Wonbri were here they could look for the rock-pool round the cliff; there's while anyway. But the boys ... the morning after Jambawal passed they set off to swim to the town. They wouldn't listen to me. They should

---

2 **to quiver** to shake – 16 **to clutch** to hold s.th. tightly – 17 **clear away** all the way – 20 **Mopoke** person's name; Australian night bird – 23 **lingo** language spoken by a certain group, not easily understood by others – 28 **rags** old, torn clothes – 35 **while** *here:* period of time

know better than to poke their noses into the white man's stinking mess. But they went.

After the night of the storm even the whites must have learned that Jambawal is stronger than any of us, that to harm him or his people is to risk his anger. The white man may have guns, and dynamite to blast the rocks, but Jambawal is the mightiest of all.

It's a hard climb up here, with the sun sitting on my head. Later in the day, or early in the morning would be easier, but by then my thirst will pin me down. Malug might hold on a little longer. I left my shirt, soaked in sea water, around his head but it might be hours before I get back with my billy full of fresh water. Poor bugger—he's held on, in spite of what he must be suffering for so long; I hope he lasts till I get back.

What a mess! The town looks like a huge rubbish dump; the higher I climb the more I can see. The airport is like a beehive; busier than it was during the war. The rescue work must have begun very early yesterday for the runways are clear and planes are flying in and out flashing like spears. The whites are pretty quick to fight for their own kind. The help is even more than the airport can take, for some planes, sweeping around the sky, can't land and drop great boxes to parachute down from their silver bellies. There's nothing much left to block my view. Even the power poles have gone, so I've got such a good view I can see those boxes bounce as they hit the ground. And look at that! The monument in Freedom Square still stands, and I can see it even better now the trees around have been levelled. Captain Cook is still riding the stone waves to the shore, as safe as he was in the war when bombs flattened everything around him. That's when I should have gone to Bralgu, with my father and the rest of our people. I've stayed too long.

I can see Flat Island from here, half sunk in the mist at the head of the bay. They don't have a leper colony there any more, but it was there before the war. Everyone on that island was black except the boss and the nurses, but though I've tried for years to remember those white people I can't call to mind one face, one word, even a glance. Maybe there wasn't a memory worth keeping. I do remember the Jap planes, though, and the bombs falling—that's when the whites took off in their boat and left us there. We never saw any of them again.

---

11 **billy** *(Aust.)* metal can or pot – **poor bugger** *(slang) armer Kerl* – 15 **beehive** *Bienenstock* – 24 **monument** statue in memory of a person or event – 25 **to level** to make flat – 31 **leper** person suffering from leprosy *(Lepra)*

My father must have been very tall. I can't remember how he looked, but if I close my eyes I can see myself riding on my father's head as he walked through the water from Flat Island to the mainland. It was low tide I suppose, but very few made it. Drowning was better than the slow and helpless death the island offered, though, for the whites came no more with food and water. Starve or drown, you end the same.

What a ruin the town is after Jambawal's rage. I suppose they'll keep the blacks away as they did before—after the air raid we walked a hundred miles around the bay only to be turned away without even a billy of tea for our trouble. My father didn't see it, though. We left him buried in the mud of the mangroves, and I held another's hand as we walked away.

It's very steep just here: I'd better watch my step. One slip and I'll end in the quarry so far below. You'd think the whites must eat rocks, they're so keen to dig them out and carry them away. Cook and his dinghy are high on such huge boulders that I wonder how they could have been moved into the town; to roll such rocks would take the sweat of hundreds of prisoners.

I wish I could hurry; I must have water soon. My mouth is already dry—perhaps I won't reach the pool. There are no leaves or grasses to squeeze for a drop or two of moisture ... if I could find a frog buried in the sand there'd be water in his belly; a cut in the bark of a bottle tree gives a man a drink—but here are only rocks for company and no chance to wet my tongue.

The ridge has been cut down close to the sea here, as if a monster had risen out of the water to take a great bite from the land. The white man is so rock-hungry he will soon have moved the whole island away—and such a lot of work has been done by me, swinging a hammer. For years the white man has been bringing me back here to the island, and often has kept me beyond the time of my sentence. It doesn't matter any more, though; I've nowhere much to go when they set me free. The first time they locked me up ... yes, I drank the water cascading over the boulders under Cook's dinghy. The statue made a fine shade to rest in, but I hardly had time to stretch out before a policeman grabbed me. I tried to explain that at the same spot had been

---

4 **to drown** to die in water – 6 **to starve** to die of hunger – 12 **mangrove** tropical tree growing in or near salt water – 15 **quarry** ['kwɒrɪ] *Steinbruch* – 17 **dinghy** ['dɪŋgɪ] small rowing-boat – **boulder** ['bəʊldə] very large, rounded rock – 26 **ridge** long, narrow stretch of higher land  – 31 **sentence** *here:* amount of time to be spent in gaol

## 58  Anon., Jambawal the Thunder Man

the sacred waterhole of my tribe, the Larrakeah people—all blackfellows, and even some of the first white men knew that. But the policeman thought I was drunk and dragged me away.

The sun is so hot and my mouth is quite dry—I'd better rest a while. See how hard the whites are working to bring their ruined town to life. They've raised flags above the piles of rubbish but the coloured rags hang down, and only move a little now and then in the breeze.

A mob of people comes spilling toward the beach, and not far ahead of the crowd races a blackfellow, running for his life. He drops the tins of food he carried, but the whites are not satisfied; they are after the man, not the food he stole. He's heading this way. Maybe ... yes, it's Wonbri. It looks as if he'll make it—he's jumped off the rocks into the sea, and the mob of whites is left behind, shouting. Wonbri's safe ... but there's a gunshot. There must be a policeman there on the beach; I can't see but I can hear the gun a second time and the cheering from the crowd. Wonbri has disappeared, but a loaf of bread still floats on the water, breaking apart as it soaks up the sea.

A convoy of ships is sailing up the harbour from the entrance toward the wharf. The whites are quick to the rescue with food and machines, and the wound on the city will soon begin to heal. Even Jambawal can't chase these men back to their own country.

There, on the other side of the bay, the setting sun is shining on Mission Beach. I always hoped—if they let me go away from here—to live there in the native settlement hidden in the thick bush, and sheltered by Banyan trees. The whites call it Half Way, and certainly it stands somewhere between the tribe and the town. It would be ... but no; it's gone too. Jambawal has wiped away even that. The huts are gone, and the Banyan trees; the beach, littered with corrugated iron, paper and rags looks strange and ugly. The mess has reached this side of the bay, too, and the body of a child lies half-buried in the sand. It will be a long time before the white man's boats come this way.

That pool of water ... it used to be here, just below those boulders, and held a little water after rain when all else had dried on those rocky slopes. The white man and his dynamite have been here since I last climbed the peak, though, and where the pool should be is a heap of shattered rock. I might have known that it couldn't survive the white man's ruin—just as the sacred caves and tribal places have been spoiled wherever his hand has lain.

---

1 **sacred** of great religious significance; holy – 19 **wharf** [wɔːf] *Kai* – 28 **corrugated iron** *Wellblech* – 37 **cave** large hole in the side of a hill – 38 **to spoil** to ruin

Yet ... yes, there it is; water seeping from a crack deep in shadow, sliding across the smooth surface of the rock and only showing itself as it drips, now and then, from the end of a crooked twig.
    Jambawal has left me behind again, in a strange country which
5 ceased to be mine long ago.

1 **to seep** to flow slowly – **crack** *Riß* – 3 **crooked** not straight – **twig** small, thin branch – 5 **to cease** to stop

### Notes

*"Jambawal the Thunder Man" originates from western Arnhem Land (northern Australia), home of the Larrakeah, an Aboriginal people. The story appeared anonymously in a journal called* Identity *in October, 1975. Founded in 1971,* Identity *contained literary and other articles of political and cultural interest, written both by and for Aborigines and Torres Strait Islanders, who are the original, i.e. indigenous, people of Australia. For a number of years* Identity *was that country's most important indigenous publication.*
*On Christmas Day (25th December), 1974, "Cyclone Tracy" razed the city of Darwin to the ground. The treatment of the Aborigines and Torres Strait Islanders by some white people following the cyclone was very harsh. "Jambawal the Thunder Man" clearly mirrors these events.*

# Summary and Teaching Notes

## Summary

The narrator, an Aborigine, is a prisoner in an island gaol. He relates how Jambawal—whom the whites call Cyclone—has ravaged the nearby town on the mainland. He has hoped this would happen and has been calling on Jambawal to come, for the white men have taken the black man's land and disfigured it. The whites have cut the Aborigines off from the places of their ancestors, thus strangling their cultural and spiritual expression.

As he surveys the disaster, the narrator chooses to stay by his wounded companion Malug, whom he has rescued from a mass of stones and concrete blocks. Jambawal struck at night, wrecking not only the nearby town, but also the gaol. The other three prisoners have left the island swimming, trying to escape. Realizing that Malug needs water, the narrator reluctantly leaves him in quest of a distant pool. As he climbs higher he sees the wreckage and notices how the white men are energetically setting about repairing the damage. He remembers a Japanese air-raid during the war, on Flat Island, from where the white men fled in their boats, leaving the black men to their own fate. They were forced to walk from the island to the mainland. The narrator, then a small child, survived, but his father drowned with many others.

Continuing his way up in search of water, the narrator recalls how he was first arrested and gaoled for drinking from the fountain at Cook's statue, where long ago the waterhole of his tribe had been. He then witnesses a violent incident. A black man, one of his fellow prisoners, is being chased by a howling mob for having stolen some food. He tries to flee by diving into the sea and swimming away, but he is gunned down. The mob cheers.

New supplies arrive. The whites will be able to continue living on the black man's land; even Jambawal cannot chase them back to their own country.

The narrator finally reaches the spot where the pool used to exist. Dynamite has virtually destroyed it. Only a few drops seep through. The Aborigine bitterly realizes his solitude in a country that is no longer his.

# Teaching Notes

## 1. Structure

### I Jambawal has struck (**53** 1–**54** 6)

*1. What do we learn in the first four paragraphs about the situation, the narrator and Jambawal the Thunder Man?*
*Situation*
A coastal town in Australia has been destroyed by a cyclone. There is not a tree or a pole left standing. All the buildings have been smashed. The white inhabitants are coming back.
*Narrator*
He is an Aboriginal prisoner in an island goal. At the time of the story he is watching the people in the destroyed town and predicting its regrowth. For him the destruction was caused by a supernatural force, Jambawal the Thunder Man, whom the narrator had called. He remembers what life was like before the whites came (**53** 24–**54** 6).
*Jambawal*
– is visible in the form of a cyclone (**53** 7)
– has come across the sea to the mainland from Bralgu (**53** 14–15)
– has come in rage (**53** 15) in answer to the prisoner's cries (**53** 13); one can sing and dance (pray) to him (**53** 18), and he will definitely come "someday" (**53** 13)
– has come to help his people, to overcome the whites following their desecration of Aboriginal land (**53** 22–**54** 6)

*2. How does the narrator feel about Jambawal's deed?*
On the one hand he is glad that he made it at last, and he admires Jambawal's performance ("a pretty good try" **53** 8). On the other hand, he is sorry Jambawal came late, because the whites have already destroyed the black man's land. To a certain extent he blames himself for not having called to Jambawal more often (**53** 21).

*3. What does the reader learn about the religous background of this Aboriginal people?*

Their religion is an ancestor cult. There are sacred places like the waterhole in which the spirit of an ancestor resides, and the trampled space where the people danced to call for rain. The black man lives close to nature, together with the spirits. Because the spirits are in the land, Aboriginal people respect and care for it ("please don't disturb" **53** 26). Ancestors seem to live on in plants and animals: the emu was once a black woman, the banyan tree was planted by Djanggawul. An Aborigine is never alone because the spirits of the ancestors are with him or her.

*4. How does the Aboriginal narrator characterize the whites?*
– They are an eager mob (**53** 3).
– They are clever: there is no way to outwit them (**53** 6–7).
– They have bulldozed the black man's land, but what they have built on it is ugly and strange (note the juxtaposition of the terms "forest" and "concrete and steel" **53** 5).
– They are greedy, taking every last corner of the land (**54** 4–6), making it difficult for Aboriginal people to call on their ancestors. (The concept of the possession of land is foreign to Aboriginal thinking.)

## II The narrator's four fellow prisoners and Jambawal's might (**54** 7–**56** 6)

*1. What information is the reader given about the other gaol inmates?*
*Malug* is unconscious, buried under a heap of concrete and stones (**55** 11–19). His moving lips indicate that he wants water (**55** 29–31). The narrator half pities, half envies Malug for being near death (**54** 26–27).
*Mopoke* is a big, tall fellow who speaks very little English (**55** 20–22) and whose tribal language the narrator himself does not understand. He has been in the gaol only a few days (**55** 22–23). Apparently he drowned and is now in Bralgu, in the Dreaming (**55** 24–28).
*Tommy and Wonbri,* two young prisoners (**54** 7–8), set off to swim to the mainland although the narrator warned them not to "poke their noses into the white man's stinking mess" (**56** 1–2).

*2. How does Jambawal demonstrate that he is angry and mighty?*
He struck at night, surprising and frightening the whites. The noise he made was louder than ever before. The earth trembled "like a beaten snake" (**55** 2). Even the black men were not spared when they got in Jambawal's way (**54** 28–29).

*3. What stylistic devices are used to emphasize Jambawal's anger and power?*
There are metaphors (Jambawal's voice) and similes (the earth trembling like a beaten snake, the walls sliding down "like a rotten fence" **55** 5). In the final paragraph of part II, there is a clear progression: stronger, guns, dynamite, but the climax is Jambawal, the mightiest of all. Ironically, such a comparison of three items, of which the third is by far the strongest, can be found often in the Bible the whites carry around (**54** 34)—cf. Psalm 20:7 "Some trust in chariots, and some in horses; but we will remember [rely on] the name of the Lord our God". In our story it is Jambawal who is mightiest and not the God of the whites. The author may well be alluding to Biblical expressions here.


### III The narrator's observations and thoughts during his climb (**56** 7–**58** 3)

Despite the difficulties ahead of him, the narrator finally decides to climb up the hill in search of water.

*Why does he do this?*
He sympathizes with Malug, trying to alleviate his suffering.
*Before interpreting* the narrator's observations of the whites, the students should find out who Captain Cook was, in order to appreciate the symbolic value of Captain Cook in this story.
*Secondly* they should gather the information about Cook's monument contained in this part of the story:
– His statue in Freedom Square still stands in spite of the war and the cyclone.
– His statue stands on huge boulders which were moved by the efforts of many prisoners, who were no doubt black like the narrator.

- His statue was erected on the very spot where the narrator was first arrested, the site of a sacred waterhole.

*In a third step* the students should consider the symbolic significance of the statue:

- The fact that Cook's statue stands in "Freedom Square" symbolizes a paradox in Australian history: while former convicts were finally able to obtain their freedom after serving in Australia, Aboriginal people suffered the loss of freedom when Cook landed and white settlement began. For them it is bitterly ironic that Cook should be placed in Freedom Square.
- Cook's "steadfastness" is symbolic of the invincible rule of the whites. There is no hope for the Aborigines. There is no hope even for the land itself, because the whites are so "rock-hungry" that they will not stop before the whole island has been moved away (**57** 28–29).
- As far as the narrator himself is concerned, Cook's statue was the reason for his arrest (**57** 33–36). He realizes that there is no hope for him as an individual: he remembers that his father is dead, his people are dead, he has nowhere to go. Cook's statue thus symbolizes his captivity and hopelessness.

During his climb the narrator observes the whites and draws conclusions: the whites are terribly busy, but only for themselves; they will not do anything to help the blacks. He also remembers the Japanese air-raid, when the whites on Flat Island deserted in their boats, leaving the blacks to their fate, and the incident after the air-raid, when the blacks were turned away.

The narrator's climb gives the author the chance to describe both the present scene and the historical development.


**IV Jambawal's failure to banish the whites, and the narrator's loneliness** (**58** 4–end)

*1. The first part of this section is full of action. How does the author manage to make this action come alive for the reader?*

As in much of this story the narrator addresses the reader directly ("See how hard..." **58** 5). We are watching the scene with him, seeing what he sees. The broken sentences ("Maybe ... yes, it's Wonbri"; "Wonbri's safe ... but there's a gunshot") create suspense. The story reads like a running commentary.

**2. What do we find out about the whites, Jambawal and the narrator in this last part of the story?**

*The whites*
– They rebuild their town, raising flags in order to show that this is their land and that they have triumphed over natural disasters.
– They do not care about the Aboriginal settlement, leaving the ruins, the litter and even the body of a child.
– They shoot a black man, the narrator's fellow prisoner, for having stolen some food.
– They have not only spoiled the sacred caves and tribal places, but they have even blown up the pool of water, thus showing their ruthlessness and lack of concern for the Aborigines.

*Jambawal*
– He is not almighty: he cannot chase the white men back to their own country.
– In his rage he did not differentiate between the white man's town and the black man's settlement.
– Again he has deserted the narrator.

*The narrator*
– His hope of finding a place to live was destroyed by Jambawal.
– His hope of finding water was destroyed by the whites.
– Is there any hope in the few drops of water?

**3. *This section prepares for the conclusion by bringing a number of things to a close. What are they?***
– The question of Wonbri's whereabouts is resolved; he dies.
– The disaster is ending: "the wound on the city will soon begin to heal" (**58** 20).
– The sun is setting (**58** 22).
– The narrator's hope of living at Mission Beach is dashed (**58** 27).

*The last sentence*—a kind of epilogue— suggests that there is no hope at all. It deserves being examined almost word by word:
– "Jambawal"—is he still the protector?
– "has left"—forsaken
– "me"—his friend who prayed to him

- "behind"—on this island, alone
- "strange country"—foreign, alien
- "ceased to be mine"—Whose fault? Why? No reason given.
- "long ago"—The narrator is left behind with a sense of abandonment and helplessness.

## 2. Style

*What stylistic devices are used in the story, and to what purpose?*
Here are some examples:
- flashbacks: Flat Island (**56** 30–**57** 7). These provide background.
- Imagery: e.g. metaphors ("forest of concrete and steel" **53** 5) and similes ("island peak ... like an ant-hill" **53** 17)
- alliteration: "roll, rattle and roar" **53** 4
- rhyme: raised flags—coloured rags (**58** 6)
- cut-off sentences: "But the boys..." (**55** 35). These increase suspense.

## 3. For further discussion

*1. Try to describe the tone of the story (optimistic, pessimistic, cynical, hopeful...). Does it change as the story progresses? Give examples.*

*2. Discuss the effects of the conversational style used in the story.*

## 4. For further study

*1. Try to find information on contemporary Aboriginal culture (cf. Perspectives 14 Australia, Klettbuch 51374, Teacher's Book 513741).*

William Saroyan

# The Hummingbird that Lived through Winter

Sometimes even instinct is overpowered by individuality—in creatures other than men, I mean. In men instinct is supposed to be controlled, but whether or not it ever actually is I leave to others. At any rate, the fundamental instinct of most—or all—creatures is to live.
5 Each form of life has an instinctive technique of defense against other forms of life, as well as against the elements. What happens to hummingbirds is something I have never found out—from actual observation or from reading. They die, that's true. And they're born somehow or other, although I have never seen a hummingbird's egg, or a young
10 hummingbird.

The mature hummingbird itself is so small that the egg must be magnificent, probably one of the most smiling little things in the world. Now, if hummingbirds come into the world through some other means than eggs, I ask the reader to forgive me. The only thing I know about
15 Agass Agasig Agassig Agazig (well, the great American naturalist) is that he once studied turtle eggs, and in order to get the information he was seeking, had to find fresh ones. This caused an exciting adventure in Boston to a young fellow who wrote about it six or seven years before I read it, when I was fourteen. I was fourteen in 1922, which goes
20 to show you how unimportant the years are when you're dealing with eggs of any kind. I envy the people who study birds, and some day I hope to find out everything that's known about hummingbirds.

I've gathered from rumor that the hummingbird travels incredible distances on incredibly little energy—what carries him, then? Spirit?
25 But the best things I know about hummingbirds are the things I've noticed about them myself; that they are on hand when the sun is out in earnest, when the blossoms are with us, and the smell of them everywhere. You can hardly go through the best kind of day without seeing

---

**hummingbird** *Kolibri* – 11 **mature** *here:* fully developed – **magnificent** wonderful, very beautiful – 16 **turtle** ['tɜːtl] *Schildkröte* – 23 **rumor** *here:* information passed on by word of mouth – 26 **in earnest** *here:* fully – 27 **blossom** flower on a tree

*Saroyan, The Hummingbird that Lived through Winter* 61

a hummingbird suspended like a little miracle in a shaft of light or over a big flower or a cluster of little ones. Or turning like gay insanity and shooting straight as an arrow toward practically nothing, for no reason, or for the reason that it's alive. Now, how can creatures such as that—so delicately magnificent and mad—possibly find time for the routine business of begetting young? Or for the exercise of instinct in self-defense? Well, however it may be, let a good day come by the grace of God, and with it will come the hummingbirds.

As I started to say, however, it appears that sometimes even instinct fails to operate in a specie. Or species. Or whatever it is. Anyhow, when all of a kind of living thing turn and go somewhere, in order to stay alive, in order to escape cold or whatever it might be, sometimes, it appears, one of them does not go. Why he does not go I cannot say. He may be eccentric, or there may be exalted reasons—specific instead of abstract passion for another of its kind—perhaps dead—or for a place. Or it may be stupidity, or stubbornness. Who can ever know?

There was a hummingbird once which in the wintertime did not leave our neighborhood in Fresno, California.

I'll tell you about it.

Across the street lived old Dikran, who was almost blind. He was past eighty and his wife was only a few years younger. They had a little house that was as neat inside as it was ordinary outside—except for old Dikran's garden, which was the best thing of its kind in the world. Plants, bushes, trees—all strong, in sweet black moist earth whose guardian was old Dikran. All things from the sky loved this spot in our poor neighborhood, and old Dikran loved *them.*

One freezing Sunday, in the dead of winter, as I came home from Sunday School I saw old Dikran standing in the middle of the street trying to distinguish what was in his hand. Instead of going into our house to the fire, as I had wanted to do, I stood on the steps of the front porch and watched the old man. He would turn around and look upward at his trees and then back to the palm of his hand. He stood in the street at least two minutes and then at last he came to me. He

---

1 **to be suspended** to hang in air – **miracle** s.th. wonderful, like a special act of God – **shaft** *here:* narrow band – 2 **cluster** small group of things close together – **insanity** complete lack of reason; madness – 6 **to beget** [-'-] *(formal)* to give birth to – 10 **species** ['spiːʃiːz] class of plants or animals – 14 **exalted** important, noble – 16 **stubbornness** unwillingness to change one's mind – 24 **moist** slightly wet, damp – 25 **guardian** keeper, protector – 28 **Sunday School** lessons in religion for children, held at a church

held his hand out, and in Armenian he said, "What is this in my hand?"

I looked.

"It is a hummingbird," I said half in English and half in Armenian. Hummingbird I said in English because I didn't know its name in Armenian.

"What is that?" old Dikran asked.

"The little bird," I said. "You know. The one that comes in the summer and stands in the air and then shoots away. The one with the wings that beat so fast you can't see them. It's in your hand. It's dying."

"Come with me," the old man said. "I can't see, and the old lady's at church. I can feel its heart beating. Is it in a bad way? Look again, once."

I looked again. It was a sad thing to behold. This wonderful little creature of summertime in the big rough hand of the old peasant. Here it was in the cold of winter, absolutely helpless and pathetic, not suspended in a shaft of summer light, not the most alive thing in the world, but the most helpless and heartbreaking.

"It's dying," I said.

The old man lifted his hand to his mouth and blew warm breath on the little thing in his hand which he could not even see. "Stay now," he said in Armenian. "It is not long till summer. Stay, swift and lovely."

We went into the kitchen of his little house, and while he blew warm breath on the bird he told me what to do.

"Put a tablespoonful of honey over the gas fire and pour it into my hand, but be sure it is not too hot."

This was done.

After a moment the hummingbird began to show signs of fresh life. The warmth of the room, the vapor of the warm honey—and, well, the will and love of the old man. Soon the old man could feel the change in his hand, and after a moment or two the hummingbird began to take little dabs of the honey.

"It will live," the old man announced. "Stay and watch."

The transformation was incredible. The old man kept his hand generously open, and I expected the helpless bird to shoot upward out of his hand, suspend itself in space, and scare the life out of me—which is exactly what happened. The new life of the little bird was magnificent. It spun about in the little kitchen, going to the window, coming

14 **to behold** to see – 16 **pathetic** sad and weak  – 30 **vapor** moisture in the air

back to the heat, suspending, circling as if it were summertime and it had never felt better in its whole life.

The old man sat on the plain chair, blind but attentive. He listened carefully and tried to see, but of course he couldn't. He kept asking about the bird, how it seemed to be, whether it showed signs of weakening again, what its spirit was, and whether or not it appeared to be restless; and I kept describing the bird to him.

When the bird was restless and wanted to go, the old man said, "Open the window and let it go."

"Will it live?" I asked.

"It is alive now and wants to go," he said. "Open the window."

I opened the window, the hummingbird stirred about here and there, feeling the cold from the outside, suspended itself in the area of the open window, stirring this way and that, and then it was gone.

"Close the window," the old man said.

We talked a minute or two and then I went home.

The old man claimed the hummingbird lived through that winter, but I never knew for sure. I saw hummingbirds again when summer came, but I couldn't tell one from the other.

One day in the summer I asked the old man.

"Did it live?"

"The little bird?" he said.

"Yes," I said. "That we gave the honey to. You remember. The little bird that was dying in the winter. Did it live?"

"Look about you," the old man said. "Do you see the bird?"

"I see humming*birds*," I said.

"Each of them is our bird," the old man said. "Each of them, each of them," he said swiftly and gently.

---

17 **to claim** to state that s.th. is true – 19 **to tell one from the other** to recognize each one individually

## Biographical Notes

*WILLIAM SAROYAN (1908–1981) was a Californian short-story writer, novelist and playwright of Armenian origin. His first collection of short stories,* The Daring Young Man on the Flying Trapeze *(1934) made him famous. Other collections of short fiction such as* My Name is Aram *followed, and in 1943 Saroyan's first novel,* The Human Comedy, *appeared. Like the story in our collection, it has to do with the experiences of children and is set in California. In 1939 his play* Time of Your Life *was awarded a Pulitzer Prize, but Saroyan refused it because the play, he said, was "no more great or good" than anything else he had written.*

# Summary and Teaching Notes

## Summary

The narrator considers that the fundamental instinct of all creatures is to live, and this applies to hummingbirds, too. He knows that they die and they are born, though he has never seen a hummingbird's egg. He knows that they travel far, that they fly around when the sun is out, when flowers are fragrant; that they are full of life and energy, delicate and fragile creatures for which he feels and expresses a great deal of tender enthusiasm.

In order to escape the cold of winter, hummingbirds emigrate. It so happens, however, for reasons unknown, that one of them stays behind. This occurs during the narrator's childhood. One freezing Sunday in winter the boy meets Dikran, an old, almost blind man, who lives across the street. Dikran is holding a small object in his hand. As he cannot see, Dikran asks what it is, and the boy explains that he is holding a hummingbird, which is dying. The old man suggests going indoors and instructs the boy to prepare some warm honey. They feed the bird with it. To their delight the hummingbird recovers. As it shows signs of wanting to escape, the old man tells the boy to open the window, and the bird flies away.

One day in the following summer the boy asks Dikran if their hummingbird has survived. The old man answers that each of the hummingbirds they can see in the garden is theirs.

# Teaching Notes

## 1. Structure

I   Introduction: The behaviour of hummingbirds seen through the narrator's eyes (**60** 1–**61** 16)
II   The story itself: A hummingbird not like the others (**61** 17–**63** 16)
III  Epilogue: The hummingbird's survival (**63** 17–end)

### I Introduction (**60** 1–**61** 16)

*1. What does the narrator say about instinct?*
- In human creatures it is supposed to be controlled (**60** 2–3).
- In other creatures it is sometimes "overpowered by individuality" (**60** 1). This is the leitmotif of the entire story.
- The main instinct "of most—or all—creatures" is to live (**60** 4).
- All creatures, therefore, have an instinctive technique of defence.

*2. What are the narrator's feelings concerning hummingbirds?*
- A certain scientific curiosity which has never been satisfied:
  How are they born?
  What are their eggs like?
- He envies people who study birds.
- He hopes to find out everything about hummingbirds.

*3. What does he know about hummingbirds?*
- From rumour: they travel incredible distances.
- From personal observation: they either hang in the sunlight or move very quickly.

*4. How does the narrator try to explain the hummingbirds' behaviour?*
- spirit?
- miracle?
- insanity?
- the grace of God?

5. *Instinct "sometimes ... fails to operate"* (**61** 9–10). *What possible reasons does the narrator give for this?*
- eccentricity
- specific passion for another of its kind or for a place
- stupidity
- stubbornness

The narrator does not attempt an answer.

6. *What does the digression about the turtle eggs add to the story?*
It adds a touch of humour, establishes the temporal setting and clearly reflects the proximity of the story to oral tradition.

7. *The story itself has not yet begun. Why such a long introduction?*
The introduction prepares the reader for the event by pointing out its significance in advance.

## II The story itself (**61** 17–**63** 16)

1. *What are we told about Dikran?*
- Armenian
- past eighty
- almost blind
- peasant with big rough hands
- loves plants and birds
- treats the small, helpless creature with warmth, generosity, love

2. *Describe the boy's part in the story.*
- He tells Dikran what he has in his hands.
- He prepares the honey.
- He describes the bird's transformation.
- He opens the window to let the bird fly away, and closes it again.

3. *Name the reasons for the bird's virtual resurrection.*
- the old man with his will, love, gentleness and experience
- the boy with his sensitivity and willingness to help
- the bird's instinct to live

103

### III Epilogue (**63** 17–end)

*1. In what way can this last section be considered an epilogue?*
An epilogue is an addition to a story, play or poem, which serves as a conclusion once the main action has finished. In "The Hummingbird" the main story ends when the bird flies away, free and alive. The subsequent section is set in the following summer and offers a conclusion to prior events—for the reader wants to know what finally happened. A satisfactory ending is necessary.
Remember that the narrator—now a mature person—is recalling the event and its "epilogue" with warm emotions, thus leaving the reader with the same feelings.

*2. What does the epilogue add to our picture of Dikran?*
It emphasizes his sensitivity and shows us that his view of nature has a spiritual element.

*3. What is the point of there being hummingbirds in the plural?*
In the epilogue the atmosphere is not the same as in the story itself. It is summertime—which suggests light, sun, life and activity—as symbolized by the hummingbirds. The question "Did the bird live?" refers back to the previous summer, but the answer concerns the present. In one bird we are confronted with hundreds.
The story itself deals mainly with events. In the epilogue more emphasis is laid on thought, reflection and the hope that life will go on: " 'Each of them is our bird' ". Note how the final word "gently" clinches the whole tone of the epilogue.

## 2. For further discussion

*1. Why does the author present Dikran as almost blind?*

*2. What does the boy learn from the old man?*

*3. What is the moral of the story?*
– Life should be protected, not destroyed.
– It is a lesson in kindness and humility.

*4. Should instinct in human beings always be controlled?*

## Sarah Orne Jewett

# A White Heron

### I

The woods were already filled with shadows one June evening, just before eight o'clock, though a bright sunset still glimmered faintly among the trunks of the trees. A little girl was driving home her cow, a plodding, dilatory, provoking creature in her behavior, but a valued companion for all that. They were going away from whatever light there was, and striking deep into the woods, but their feet were familiar with the path, and it was no matter whether their eyes could see it or not.

There was hardly a night the summer through when the old cow could be found waiting at the pasture bars; on the contrary, it was her greatest pleasure to hide herself away among the huckleberry bushes, and though she wore a loud bell she had made the discovery that if one stood perfectly still it would not ring. So Sylvia had to hunt for her until she found her, and call Co'! Co'! with never an answering Moo, until her childish patience was quite spent. If the creature had not given good milk and plenty of it, the case would have seemed very different to her owners. Besides, Sylvia had all the time there was, and very little use to make of it. Sometimes in pleasant weather it was a consolation to look upon the cow's pranks as an intelligent attempt to play hide and seek, and as the child had no playmates she lent herself to this amusement with a good deal of zest. Though this chase had been so long that the wary animal herself had given an unusual signal of her whereabouts, Sylvia had only laughed when she came upon Mistress Moolly at the swampside, and urged her affectionately homeward with a twig of birch leaves. The old cow was not inclined to wander farther; she even turned in the right direction for once as they left the pasture, and stepped along the road at a good pace. She was quite

---

**heron** *Reiher* – 3 **to plod** to walk slowly and heavily – 4 **dilatory** ['dɪlətərɪ] doing things slowly, in a delayed manner – 9 **pasture** land that has grass – 10 **huckleberry** *(AE)* blueberry – 18 **consolation** attempt to make s.o. more cheerful – **prank** childish trick – 20 **zest** energy – 21 **wary** ['weərɪ] careful – 23 **swampside** edge of an area of very wet land – **affectionately** with warm feelings – 24 **twig** small, thin branch – **birch** *Birke* – **to be inclined to do s.th.** to be in the habit of doing s.th.

## 66 Sarah Orne Jewett, A White Heron

ready to be milked now, and seldom stopped to browse. Sylvia wondered what her grandmother would say because they were so late. It was a great while since she had left home at half-past five o'clock, but everybody knew the difficulty of making this errand a short one. Mrs Tilley had chased the hornéd torment too many summer evenings herself to blame any one else for lingering, and was only thankful as she waited that she had Sylvia, nowadays, to give such valuable assistance. The good woman suspected that Sylvia loitered occasionally on her own account; there never was such a child for straying about out-of-doors since the world was made! Everybody said that it was a good change for a little maid who had tried to grow for eight years in a crowded manufacturing town, but as for Sylvia herself, it seemed as if she never had been alive at all before she came to live at the farm. She thought often with wistful compassion of a wretched geranium that belonged to a town neighbor.

" 'Afraid of folks,' " old Mrs Tilley said to herself, with a smile, after she made the unlikely choice of Sylvia from her daughter's houseful of children, and was returning to the farm. " 'Afraid of folks,' they said! I guess she won't be troubled no great with 'em up to the old place!" When they reached the door of the lonely house and stopped to unlock it, and the cat came to purr loudly, and rub against them, a deserted pussy, indeed, but fat with young robins, Sylvia whispered that this was a beautiful place to live in, and she never should wish to go home.

The companions followed the shady woodroad, the cow taking slow steps and the child very fast ones. The cow stopped long at the brook to drink, as if the pasture were not half a swamp, and Sylvia stood still and waited, letting her bare feet cool themselves in the shoal water, while the great twilight moths struck softly against her. She waded on through the brook as the cow moved away, and listened to the thrushes with a heart that beat fast with pleasure. There was a stirring in the great boughs overhead. They were full of little birds and

---

1 **to browse** [braʊz] to feed on grass – 4 **errand** short trip undertaken to do a job for s.o. – 5 **torment** ['--] s.th. which causes pain – 6 **to linger** to stay longer than necessary – 8 **to loiter** to walk up and down aimlessly – 9 **to stray** *here:* to wander – 14 **wistful** rather sad – **compassion** feeling of pity – **wretched** ['retʃɪd] miserable – 19 **no great** *(dial.)* a lot – **up to** *(dial.)* up at – 21 **deserted** left alone – 22 **robin** *Rotkehlchen* – 27 **brook** small stream – 28 **shoal** *here:* shallow – 29 **twilight** the time when the light fades after sunset – 31 **thrush** *Drossel* – 32 **bough** [baʊ] large branch

beasts that seemed to be wide awake, and going about their world, or else saying good night to each other in sleepy twitters. Sylvia herself felt sleepy as she walked along. However, it was not much farther to the house, and the air was soft and sweet. She was not often in the woods so late as this, and it made her feel as if she were a part of the gray shadows and the moving leaves. She was just thinking how long it seemed since she first came to the farm a year ago, and wondering if everything went on in the noisy town just the same as when she was there; the thought of the great red-faced boy who used to chase and frighten her made her hurry along the path to escape from the shadow of the trees.

Suddenly this little woods-girl is horror-stricken to hear a clear whistle not very far away. Not a bird's-whistle, which would have a sort of friendliness, but a boy's whistle, determined, and somewhat aggressive. Sylvia left the cow to whatever sad fate might await her, and stepped discreetly aside into the bushes, but she was just too late. The enemy had discovered her, and called out in a very cheerful and persuasive tone, "Halloa, little girl, how far is it to the road?" and trembling Sylvia answered almost inaudibly, "A good ways."

She did not dare to look boldly at the tall young man, who carried a gun over his shoulder, but she came out of her bush and again followed the cow, while he walked alongside.

"I have been hunting for some birds," the stranger said kindly, "and I have lost my way, and need a friend very much. Don't be afraid," he added gallantly. "Speak up and tell me what your name is, and whether you think I can spend the night at your house, and go out gunning early in the morning."

Sylvia was more alarmed than before. Would not her grandmother consider her much to blame? But who could have foreseen such an accident as this? It did not seem to be her fault, and she hung her head as if the stem of it were broken, but managed to answer "Sylvy," with much effort when her companion again asked her name.

Mrs Tilley was standing in the doorway when the trio came into view. The cow gave a loud moo by way of explanation.

"Yes, you'd better speak up for yourself, you old trial! Where'd she tucked herself away this time, Sylvy?" But Sylvia kept an awed

---

15 **fate** what happens in the future – 19 **inaudibly** [ɪnˈɔːdəblɪ] not loud enough to be heard – 20 **boldly** without fear – 30 **accident** *here:* s.th. unforeseen, a chance event – 31 **stem** *here:* neck – 35 **trial** cause of annoyance – 36 **tucked** *here:* hidden – **awed** fearful and full of respect

68 *Sarah Orne Jewett, A White Heron*

silence; she knew by instinct that her grandmother did not comprehend the gravity of the situation. She must be mistaking the stranger for one of the farmer-lads of the region.

The young man stood his gun beside the door, and dropped a lumpy game-bag beside it; then he bade Mrs Tilley good evening, and repeated his wayfarer's story, and asked if he could have a night's lodging.

"Put me anywhere you like," he said. "I must be off early in the morning, before day; but I am very hungry, indeed. You can give me some milk at any rate, that's plain."

"Dear sakes, yes," responded the hostess, whose long-slumbering hospitality seemed to be easily awakened. "You might fare better if you went out to the main road a mile or so, but you're welcome to what we've got. I'll milk right off, and you make yourself at home. You can sleep on husks or feathers," she proffered graciously. "I raised them all myself. There's good pasturing for geese just below here toward the ma'sh. Now step round and set a plate for the gentleman, Sylvy!" And Sylvia promptly stepped. She was glad to have something to do, and she was hungry herself.

It was a surprise to find so clean and comfortable a little dwelling in this New England wilderness. The young man had known the horrors of its most primitive housekeeping, and the dreary squalor of that level of society which does not rebel at the companionship of hens. This was the best thrift of an old-fashioned farmstead, though on such a small scale that it seemed like a hermitage. He listened eagerly to the old woman's quaint talk, he watched Sylvia's pale face and shining gray eyes with ever growing enthusiasm, and insisted that this was the best supper he had eaten for a month, and afterward the new-made friends sat down in the doorway together while the moon came up.

Soon it would be berry-time, and Sylvia was a great help at picking. The cow as a good milker, though a plaguy thing to keep track of, the hostess gossiped frankly, adding presently that she had buried four children, so Sylvia's mother, and a son (who might be dead) in California were all the children she had left. "Dan, my boy, was a great hand to go gunning," she explained sadly. "I never wanted for

---

2 **gravity** *(here)* seriousness – 4 **lumpy** of uneven shape, showing that s.th. is in the bag – 5 **game-bag** bag for putting animals in after hunting – 6 **wayfarer** [fɛə] traveller – 10 **long-slumbering** *here:* not used for a long time – 11 **hospitality** desire to make guests feel welcome – 14 **husk** outer skin of grain – 16 **ma'sh** marsh, very wet land – 19 **dwelling** house – 21 **squalor** ['skwɒlə] bad living conditions; dirt, misery – 24 **hermitage** ['hɜːmɪtɪdʒ] isolated place where s.o. lives alone – 25 **quaint** attractively old-fashioned – 30 **plaguy** ['pleɪgɪ] annoying

pa'tridges or gray squer'ls while he was to home. He's been a great wand'rer, I expect, and he's no hand to write letters. There, I don't blame him, I'd ha' seen the world myself if it had been so I could."

"Sylvy takes after him," the grandmother continued affectionately, after a minute's pause. "There ain't a foot o' ground she don't know her way over, and the wild creaturs counts her one o' themselves. Squer'ls she'll tame to come an' feed right out o' her hands, and all sorts o' birds. Last winter she got the jaybirds to bangeing here, and I believe she'd 'a' scanted herself of her own meals to have plenty to throw out amongst 'em, if I hadn't kep' watch. Anything but crows, I tell her, I'm willin' to help support—though Dan he had a tamed one o' them that did seem to have reason same as folks. It was round here a good spell after he went away. Dan an' his father they didn't hitch— but he never held up his head ag'n after Dan had dared him an' gone off."

The guest did not notice this hint of family sorrows in his eager interest in something else.

"So Sylvy knows all about birds, does she?" he exclaimed, as he looked around at the little girl who sat, very demure but increasingly sleepy, in the moonlight. "I am making a collection of birds myself. I have been at it ever since I was a boy." (Mrs Tilley smiled.) "There are two or three very rare ones I have been hunting for these five years. I mean to get them on my own ground if they can be found."

"Do you cage 'em up?" asked Mrs Tilley doubtfully, in response to this enthusiastic announcement.

"Oh no, they're stuffed and preserved, dozens and dozens of them," said the ornithologist, "and I have shot or snared every one myself. I caught a glimpse of a white heron a few miles from here on Saturday, and I have followed it in this direction. They have never been found in this district at all. The little white heron, it is," and he turned again to look at Sylvia with the hope of discovering that the rare bird was one of her acquaintances.

But Sylvia was watching a hop-toad in the narrow footpath.

"You would know the heron if you saw it," the stranger continued eagerly. "A queer tall white bird with soft feathers and long thin legs.

---

1 **pa'tridge** partridge *(Rebhuhn)* – **squer'l** squirrel *(Eichhörnchen)* – 7 **to tame** to train a wild animal – 8 **jaybird** *Eichelhäher* – **bangeing** *(dial.)* nesting – 9 **to scant** to do without – 13 **a good spell** quite some time – **to hitch** *here:* to get on well with s.o. – 19 **demure** quiet and shy – 26 **to stuff s.th.** to make a life-size model of s.th. by filling out its skin – 27 **ornithologist** person who studies birds – **to snare** to catch in traps – 32 **acquaintance** *Bekannte/r* – 33 **hop-toad** *Kröte*

*Sarah Orne Jewett, A White Heron*

And it would have a nest perhaps in the top of a high tree, made of sticks, something like a hawk's nest."

Sylvia's heart gave a wild beat; she knew that strange white bird, and had once stolen softly near where it stood in some bright green swamp grass, away over at the other side of the woods. There was an open place where the sunshine always seemed strangely yellow and hot, where tall, nodding rushes grew, and her grandmother had warned her that she might sink in the soft black mud underneath and never be heard of more. Not far beyond were the salt marshes just this side of the sea itself, which Sylvia wondered and dreamed much about, but never had seen, whose great voice could sometimes be heard above the noise of the woods on stormy nights.

"I can't think of anything I should like so much as to find that heron's nest," the handsome stranger was saying. "I would give ten dollars to anybody who could show it to me," he added desperately, "and I mean to spend my whole vacation hunting for it if need be. Perhaps it was only migrating, or had been chased out of its own region by some bird of prey."

Mrs Tilley gave amazed attention to all this, but Sylvia still watched the toad, not divining, as she might have done at some calmer time, that the creature wished to get to its hole under the doorstep, and was much hindered by the unusual spectators at that hour of the evening. No amount of thought, that night, could decide how many wished-for treasures the ten dollars, so lightly spoken of, would buy.

The next day the young sportsman hovered about the woods, and Sylvia kept him company, having lost her first fear of the friendly lad, who proved to be most kind and sympathetic. He told her many things about the birds and what they knew and where they lived and what they did with themselves. And he gave her a jackknife, which she thought as great a treasure as if she were a desert-islander. All day long he did not once make her troubled or afraid except when he brought down some unsuspecting singing creature from its bough. Sylvia would have liked him vastly better without his gun; she could not understand why he killed the very birds he seemed to like so much. But as the day waned, Sylvia still watched the young man with loving admiration. She had never seen anybody so charming and delightful; the

---

2 **hawk** *Habicht* – 7 **rushes** tall plants growing near water – 20 **to devine** to understand – 22 **spectator** s.o. who is watching s.th. – 25 **to hover** ['hɒvə] *here:* to move slowly, expectantly – 29 **jackknife** a large pocket-knife – 32 **unsuspecting** unaware – 33 **vastly** much – 35 **to wane** to fade – **admiration** great respect

woman's heart, asleep in the child, was vaguely thrilled by a dream of love. Some premonition of that great power stirred and swayed these young creatures who traversed the solemn woodlands with soft-footed silent care. They stopped to listen to a bird's song; they pressed forward again eagerly, parting the branches—speaking to each other rarely and in whispers; the young man going first and Sylvia following, fascinated, a few steps behind, with her gray eyes dark with excitement.

She grieved because the longed-for white heron was elusive, but she did not lead the guest, she only followed, and there was no such thing as speaking first. The sound of her own unquestioned voice would have terrified her—it was hard enough to answer yes or no when there was no need of that. At last evening began to fall, and they drove the cow home together, and Sylvia smiled with pleasure when they came to the place where she heard the whistle and was afraid only the night before.

## II

Half a mile from home, at the farther edge of the woods, where the land was highest, a great pine-tree stood, the last of its generation. Whether it was left for a boundary mark, or for what reason, no one could say; the woodchoppers who had felled its mates were dead and gone long ago, and a whole forest of sturdy trees, pines and oaks and maples, had grown again. But the stately head of this old pine towered above them all and made a landmark for sea and shore miles and miles away. Sylvia knew it well. She had always believed that whoever climbed on the top of it could see the ocean; and the little girl had often laid her hand on the great rough trunk and looked up wistfully at those dark boughs that the wind always stirred, no matter how hot and still the air might be below. Now she thought of the tree with a new excitement, for why, if one climbed it at break of day, could not one see all the world, and easily discover from whence the white heron flew, and mark the place, and find the hidden nest?

What a spirit of adventure, what wild ambition! What fancied triumph and delight and glory for the later morning when she could

---

2 **premonition** forewarning – **to sway** *here:* to influence – 3 **solemn** ['sɒləm] *here:* dark, quiet – 9 **to grieve** to feel very sad – **elusive** difficult to find or grasp – 19 **boundary** imaginary line that separates two areas of land – 20 **mate** *here:* friend – 21 **sturdy** strong, upright – **oak** *Eiche* – 22 **maple** *Ahorn* – 23 **landmark** feature of the land seen at a great distance – 32 **to fancy** *here:* to imagine

## 72  Sarah Orne Jewett, A White Heron

make known the secret! It was almost too real and too great for the childish heart to bear.

All night the door of the little house stood open and the whippoorwills came and sang upon the the very step. The young sportsman and
5 his old hostess were sound asleep, but Sylvia's great design kept her broad awake and watching. She forgot to think of sleep. The short summer night seemed as long as the winter darkness, and at last when the whippoorwills ceased, and she was afraid the morning would after all come too soon, she stole out of the house and followed the pasture
10 path through the woods, hastening toward the open ground beyond, listening with a sense of comfort and companionship to the drowsy twitter of a half-awakened bird, whose perch she had jarred in passing. Alas, if the great wave of human interest which flooded for the first time this dull little life should sweep away the satisfactions of an
15 existence heart to heart with nature and the dumb life of the forest!

There was the huge tree asleep yet in the paling moonlight, and small and silly Sylvia began with utmost bravery to mount to the top of it, with tingling, eager blood coursing the channels of her whole frame, with her bare feet and fingers, that pinched and held like bird's
20 claws to the monstrous ladder reaching up, up, almost to the sky itself. First she must mount the white oak tree that grew alongside, where she was almost lost among the dark branches and the green leaves heavy and wet with dew; a bird fluttered off its nest, and a red squirrel ran to and fro and scolded pettishly at the harmless housebreaker.
25 Sylvia felt her way easily. She had often climbed there, and knew that higher still one of the oak's upper branches chafed against the pine trunk, just where its lower boughs were set close together. There, when she made the dangerous pass from one tree to the other, the great enterprise would really begin.

30 She crept out along the swaying oak limb at last, and took the daring step across into the old pine-tree. The way was harder than she thought; she must reach far and hold fast, the sharp dry twigs caught

---

3 **whippoorwill** [ˈwɪppʊəwɪl] *Nachtschwalbe* – 5 **design** *here:* plan – 10 **to hasten** [ˈheɪsn] to hurry – 11 **drowsy** sleepy – 12 **perch** part of a branch where a bird sits – **to jar** to strike with force – 18 **tingling** prickling with excitement – **to course** to move through – 19 **frame** *here:* body – **to pinch** to squeeze between finger and thumb – 23 **dew** small drops of water that form on the ground and leaves during the night – 24 **to scold** to speak angrily with s.o. – **pettishly** getting upset at little things – 26 **to chafe** to rub against – 30 **to sway** *here:* to move with the wind – **limb** branch of a tree

## Sarah Orne Jewett, A White Heron

and held her and scratched her like angry talons, the pitch made her thin little fingers clumsy and stiff as she went around and around the tree's great stem, higher and higher upward. The sparrows and robins in the woods below were beginning to wake and twitter to the dawn, yet it seemed much lighter there aloft in the pine-tree, and the child knew she must hurry if her project were to be of any use.

The tree seemed to lengthen itself out as she went up, and to reach farther and farther upward. It was like a great main-mast to the voyaging earth; it must truly have been amazed that morning through all its ponderous frame as it felt this determined spark of human spirit wending its way from higher branch to branch. Who knows how steadily the least twigs held themselves to advantage this light, weak creature on her way! The old pine must have loved his new dependent. More than all the hawks, and bats, and moths, and even the sweet voiced thrushes, was the brave, beating heart of the solitary gray-eyed child. And the tree stood still and frowned away the winds that June morning while the dawn grew bright in the east.

Sylvia's face was like a pale star, if one had seen it from the ground, when the last thorny bough was past, and she stood trembling and tired but wholly triumphant, high in the treetop. Yes, there was the sea with the dawning sun making a golden dazzle over it, and toward that glorious east flew two hawks with slow-moving pinions. How low they looked in the air from that height when one had only seen them before far up, and dark against the blue sky. Their gray feathers were as soft as moths; they seemed only a little way from the tree, and Sylvia felt as if she too could go flying away among the clouds. Westward, the woodlands and farms reached miles and miles into the distance; here and there were church steeples, and white villages, truly it was a vast and awesome world!

The birds sang louder and louder. At last the sun came up bewilderingly bright. Sylvia could see the white sails of ships out at sea, and the clouds that were purple and rose-colored and yellow at first began to fade away. Where was the white heron's nest in the sea of green

---

1 **talon** claw of a bird of prey – **pitch** *here:* sticky substance on the tree – 2 **clumsy** moving with difficulty – 3 **sparrow** *Spatz* – 5 **aloft** high up – 10 **ponderous** heavy, large – 12 **steadily** without shaking – 14 **bat** *Fledermaus* – 16 **to frown** [fraʊn] to draw eyebrows together to express displeasure – 21 **dazzle** sudden brightness – 22 **pinion** wing or flight feather – 28 **steeple** pointed structure at the top of a church tower – 30 **bewilderingly** in a confusing way

*74 Sarah Orne Jewett, A White Heron*

branches, and was this wonderful sight and pageant of the world the only reward for having climbed to such a giddy height? Now look down again, Sylvia, where the green marsh is set among the shining birches and dark hemlocks; there where you saw the white heron once you will see him again; look, look! a white spot of him like a single floating feather comes up from the dead hemlock and grows larger, and rises, and comes close at last, and goes by the landmark pine with steady sweep of wing and outstretched slender neck and crested head. And wait! wait! do not move a foot or a finger, little girl, do not send an arrow of light and consciousness from your two eager eyes, for the heron has perched on a pine bough not far beyond yours, and cries back to his mate on the nest and plumes his feathers for the new day!

The child gives a long sigh a minute later when a company of shouting cat-birds comes also to the tree, and vexed by their fluttering and lawlessness the solemn heron goes away. She knows his secret now, the wild, light, slender bird that floats and wavers, and goes back like an arrow presently to his home in the green world beneath. Then Sylvia, well satisfied, makes her perilous way down again, not daring to look far below the branch she stands on, ready to cry sometimes because her fingers ache and her lamed feet slip. Wondering over and over again what the stranger would say to her, and what he would think when she told him how to find his way straight to the heron's nest.

"Sylvy, Sylvy!" called the busy old grandmother again and again, but nobody answered, and the small husk bed was empty and Sylvia had disappeared.

The guest waked from a dream, and remembering his day's pleasure hurried to dress himself that might it sooner begin. He was sure from the way the shy little girl looked once or twice yesterday that she had at least seen the white heron, and now she must really be made to tell. Here she comes now, paler than ever, and her worn old frock is torn and tattered, and smeared with pine pitch. The grandmother and the

---

1 **pageant** ['pædʒənt] colourful outdoor show – 2 **giddy** causing dizziness – 4 **hemlock** *Schierling* – 8 **slender** slim, thin – **crested** with feathers standing up on its head – 12 **mate** *here:* partner of the opposite sex – **to plume** to clean and arrange the feathers with the beak – 14 **cat-bird** *amerikanischer Spottdrossel* – **to vex** to annoy – 18 **perilous** very dangerous – 20 **ache** [eɪk] pain – 32 **frock** woman's or girl's dress – 33 **tattered** badly torn – **to smear** [smɪə] to cover with dirty marks

sportsman stand in the door together and question her, and the splendid moment has come to speak of the dead hemlock-tree by the green marsh.

But Sylvia does not speak after all, though the old grandmother fretfully rebukes her, and the young man's kind, appealing eyes are looking straight in her own. He can make them rich with money; he has promised it, and they are poor now. He is so well worth making happy, and he waits to hear the story she can tell.

No, she must keep silence! What is it that suddenly forbids her and makes her dumb? Has she been nine years growing and now, when the great world for the first time puts out a hand to her, must she thrust it aside for a bird's sake? The murmur of pine's green branches is in her ears, she remembers how the white heron came flying through the golden air and how they watched the sea and the morning together, and Sylvia cannot speak; she cannot tell the heron's secret and give its life away.

Dear loyalty, that suffered a sharp pang as the guest went away disappointed later in the day, that could have served and followed him and loved him as a dog loves! Many a night Sylvia heard the echo of his whistle haunting the pasture path as she came home with the loitering cow. She forgot even her sorrow at the sharp report of his gun and the sight of thrushes and sparrows dropping silent to the ground, their songs hushed and their pretty feathers stained and wet with blood. Were the birds better friends than their hunter might have been—who can tell? Whatever treasures were lost to her, woodlands and summertime, remember! Bring your gifts and graces and tell your secrets to this lonely country child!

---

4 **fretfully** in a worried way – 5 **to rebuke** to speak severely to someone – **appealing** attractive; as if if asking for s.th. – 10 **dumb** unable to speak – 11 **to thrust** to push or throw with force – 12 **murmur** ['mɜːmə] whisper – 17 **pang** sudden sharp feeling of pain

*76 Sarah Orne Jewett, A White Heron*

**Biographical Notes**

*SARAH ORNE JEWETT (1849–1909) was born in a small town in Maine. Her first story was printed in the* Atlantic Monthly *when she was nineteen. Her stories and novels are set in her native New England. They include* A Country Doctor, *a novel about a New England girl who refuses marriage so as to become a doctor.* A White Heron *is the title piece of a collection of short stories. She also wrote poems and three books for children.*

# Summary and Teaching Notes

## Summary

Sylvia, a shy nine-year-old formerly brought up in a large family in a manufacturing town, has been living for the past year with her grandmother in the depths of the country. Ever since her arrival she has loved nature. Late one evening, as she is driving back the cow to be milked, she meets a cheerful young man armed with a shotgun, who explains that he has lost his way. Although afraid of him she leads him to her grandmother's simple dwelling. There they all spend a pleasant evening, and the young man stays overnight.
The young man grows enthusiastic when he learns that Sylvia knows a lot about birds. He explains that he is an ornithologist who shoots birds to have them stuffed so as to add them to his already large collection. He tells them that he has caught a glimpse of a white heron and is very keen to find its nest, offering a ten-dollar reward to anybody who can show it to him.
Sylvia thinks she knows about this bird, but she prefers to say nothing.
The next day Sylvia accompanies the cheerful young man.
Despite her fascination and emerging love she cannot understand why he should shoot and kill the birds he seems to like so much.
They fail to locate the heron's nest and return home at nightfall.
During the night Sylvia decides to climb to the top of a gigantic, century-old pine-tree to try to discover the exact whereabouts of the heron's nest.
She steals out of the house at first light and struggles up to the top of the tree. She looks in the direction of a marsh, where she has previously seen the white heron.
Suddenly, as the sun begins to rise, the heron appears, flies towards her and perches on a bough below her. When disturbed by other birds it flies away and returns to its nest and mate in the swamp below. Sylvia now knows where the white heron has its nest and descends fully prepared to tell the young man.

However, despite all the tempting perspectives such a revelation would offer, she remains stubbornly silent, for she feels she cannot divulge the white heron's secret and forfeit its life. The hunter goes away disappointed.

# Teaching Notes

## 1. Structure

The story is divided into parts I (**65** 1–**71** 16) and II (**71** 17–end).

*1. What time span is covered by the two parts respectively?*
I One whole day. Structural unity in Part I is created by the reference to the "place where she heard the whistle and was afraid only the night before" (**71** 15–16) at the end.

II The ensuing night and the following morning.

*2. Try to subdivide the two parts.*
The following is a suggestion:

I  a  Introduction: Sylvia (**65** 1–**67** 11)
   b  The meeting with the stranger (**67** 12–**70** 24)
   c  The day's outing (**70** 25–**71** 16)

II a  The ascent of the pine-tree (**71** 17–**74** 24)
   b  Sylvia's refusal (**74** 25–**75** 16)
   c  An epilogue (**75** 17–end)

*3. Consider Sylvia's role in the story. What differing aspects of her personality are conveyed in the two parts?*
Sylvia remains the main character throughout.

I Sylvia is passive; first she is fearful, then full of admiration.

II Sylvia asserts her personality. She discovers a new world which leads her to make decisions and assume responsibility. From now on she is a different person.

*4. List the constellations of characters in each part.*
I Sylvia and her grandmother form a unity.
 The stranger joins them and speaks of the white heron he would like to catch. The heron links the characters of the story. This can be illustrated graphically.

```
Sylvia + grandmother ┐
                     ├─ heron
         stranger    ┘
```

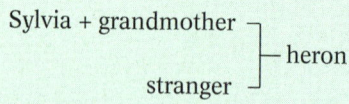

The white heron is at first a mysterious, elusive image—almost mythical, not physically present.

II Sylvia leaves the group in order to find out about the bird herself. Both grandmother and stranger are excluded from Sylvia's new experience.

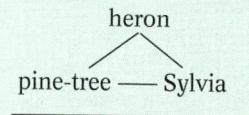

```
            heron
           /    \
          /      \
pine-tree ────── Sylvia
```
---
grandmother + stranger

Sylvia and the pine-tree form a very close union that resembles a personal relationship. The pine-tree speaks to Sylvia like a real person. She also feels at one with the heron ("...they watched the sea and the morning together" **75** 14).

In the following, each part of the story will be examined.

### I a Introduction (**65** 1–**67** 11)

The story starts with a description of the immediate situation and the main character (**65** 1–7).

*1. What do we learn about Sylvia in these first lines?*
Since the cow is a "valued companion", Sylvia must lead a lonely life (**65** 4–5). She is very familiar with the countryside.

The immediate situation is then placed in its larger context (**65** 8 ff.), and the author employs the device of flashback (**66** 10–19) to show where Sylvia has come from. We are then led back into the situation at hand, though Sylvia's reminiscences (**67** 6–11) provide further background and a link to coming events (cf. the "red-faced boy who used to chase and frighten her").

*2. Describe Sylvia's feelings about living in the country and her relationship to nature. Find examples.*

Her very first impression: it was "a beautiful place to live in" (**66** 23). See also:
- "but their feet were familiar with the path" (**65** 6–7)
- "letting her bare feet cool themselves in the shoal water ... against her" (**66** 28–29)
- She "listened to the thrushes with a heart that beat fast with pleasure" (**66** 30–31)
- "it made her feel as if she were a part of the gray shadows and the moving leaves" (**67** 5–6)

*3. The cow is personified and described in very human terms. Find examples and try to explain what effect this produces.*
The cow is introduced in the first paragraph as a "plodding, dilatory, provoking creature". It is referred to with the pronoun "she" rather than "it" and is credited with will and intelligence (**65** 9–12). She is Sylvia's companion.
The cow's name is "Mistress Moolly" (note the onomatopoeia and the association with "Molly", a girl's name). This personification (anthropomorphism) adds a humorous touch and helps create a light-hearted atmosphere at the start of the story. It also heightens the sense of innocence surrounding Sylvia, who is the cow's companion.

*4. What impressions do we gain of Sylvia's grandmother from these first paragraphs?*
The "good woman" (**66** 8), Mrs Tilley, has chosen Sylvia out of all her grandchildren to live with her on the farm, knowing that Sylvia was shy of other people (**66** 16–19). She is understanding and does not blame Sylvia for loitering occasionally "on her own account" (**66** 8–9). She seems a cheerful person ("with a smile" **66** 16) and is grateful for Sylvia's "valuable assistance" (**66** 7–8).

*5. Examine the point of view between **66** 8 ("The good woman") and **66** 15 ("a town neighbor").*
The narrator is positioned outside the story, revealing the thoughts of the characters involved (omniscient point of view). In these lines the narrator reveals first the grandmother's thoughts, then those of Sylvia ("but as for Sylvia herself...").

### I b  Encounter with the stranger (**67** 12–**70** 24)

The section begins with an unexpected change to the present tense. After the slow-moving introduction, the reader is startled ("Suddenly..."), just as Sylvia is "horror-stricken" (**67** 12).

*1. What is the effect of such terms as "determined, and somewhat aggressive" (**67** 14–15) and "The enemy" (**67** 16–17)?*
These create suspense, introducing an element of drama. The reader can identify with Sylvia's fear. Such threatening terms also serve to heighten the sense of relief felt by the reader when "the enemy" turns out to be a cheerful young man who speaks kindly and even in a gentlemanly manner to Sylvia. Nevertheless Sylvia remains shy, trembling and speaking "almost inaudibly" (**67** 19). Upon arrival at the farmstead she hangs her head (**67** 30) and keeps "an awed silence" (**67** 36–**68** 1).

*2. Make a summary of what follows after the stranger has appeared (**67** 16–**70** 24).*
The summary should include the following (but keep it brief!):
– The young man's plans and wishes; his reception at Mrs Tilley's house and his feelings as a result;
– The grandmother's mention of Uncle Dan;
– The stranger's interest in the heron and in Sylvia's knowledge; his offer of a reward.

*3. Consider the similarities and differences between Dan and the stranger.*
Both go gunning, both like to wander. Dan shot animals for food (**68** 33–**69** 1); the young stranger shoots birds as trophies (**69** 26).

*4. What does the heron mean to the stranger? Why is he so eager to find it?*
Note that the stranger ignores Mrs Tilley's "hint of family sorrows" (**69** 16) in his quest for knowledge of the heron. He has been hunting this and other rare birds for five years already (**69** 22). His collection of birds is something like a life's work (**69** 20–21). His offer of a reward and his willingness to hunt all summer for the heron (**70** 13–16) testify to his enthusiasm.

*5. Sylvia knows something about the white heron and its nest (**70** 3–12). Why does she keep quiet about it?*
The description of Sylvia's encounter with the "strange white bird" indicates that it was a special experience for her. Students could pick out elements of the description that suggest the place itself has an almost mystical quality (the sunlight, the black mud, the dream-like sound of the ocean). The heron is part of Sylvia's private world. Perhaps, too, she is still afraid of the stranger.

### I c  The day's outing: Sylvia and the stranger (**70** 25–**71** 16)

*1. Pick out phrases that describe Sylvia's feelings toward the young man.*
Students should note how Sylvia's feelings towards the stranger change, how she becomes aware of the contradictions in his character, why she is under his spell and charm and feels excited nevertheless.
- "lost her first fear of the friendly lad" (**70** 26)
- "kind and sympathetic" (**70** 27)
- She treasures his gift (**70** 29–30).
- dislike of his shooting birds (**70** 32–34)
- "loving admiration" (**70** 35–36)
- "charming and delightful" (**70** 36)
- premonition of love (**71** 1–2)
- excitement (**71** 7–8)

*2. How does Sylvia become aware of the contradictions in his character?*
"...she could not understand..." (**70** 33–34). Sylvia senses that the young man's love of nature does not match his destruction of it.

*3. What is significant about the sentence "she did not lead the guest, she only followed" (**71** 9–10)?*
It shows her subordination to his will, just as she would never have spoken first. At the same time her silence and submission means she is keeping back her knowledge of the heron's whereabouts.

### II a  The ascent of the pine-tree (71 17–74 23)

*1. How is the pine-tree described?*
Students should not only refer to the adjectives ("great", "stately", "old", "huge"), but they should realize how the tree seems to develop human features, reactions and characteristics (personification), e.g.:
- "the last of its generation" (**71** 18)
- "its mates" (**71** 20)
- "the stately head" (**71** 22)
- "it must truly have been amazed" (**73** 9)
- "felt this determined spark" (**73** 10)
- The old pine-tree must have loved his new dependent" (**73** 13)
- "the tree stood still and frowned away the winds" (**73** 16)

*2. Explain the following similes:*
- "... the sharp dry twigs caught and held her ... like angry talons" (**72** 32–**73** 1)
- "It was like a great main-mast to the voyaging earth" (**73** 8–9)

*3. After studying Sylvia's struggle up to the top of the tree, students could analyse Sylvia's physical and emotional state:*
"trembling and tired but wholly triumphant" (**73** 19–20) and "Sylvia felt as if she too could go flying" (**73** 25–26). At this point the narrator switches to present tense and speaks directly to Sylvia: "Now look down again, Sylvia" (**74** 2–3).

*4. What is the effect and significance of this sudden change in the narration?*
It could seem to be an inner voice speaking to Sylvia.

*5. Find examples of poetic use of language in this section* (**74** 2–12).
- Exclamations: "look, look!" and "wait! wait!"
- Simile: "like a single floating feather"
- Metaphor: "an arrow of light and consciousness"
- Alliteration: "floating feather", "comes close", "steady sweep", "eager eyes", "perched on a pine bough"
- Copious use of adjectives

If time allows, the teacher could draw students' attention to the change of style from the lines just examined to **74** 13–23. Though present tense is still employed, the sentences are no longer in the imperative. The atmosphere is thus calmer. There are no exclamations. This section is a kind of denouement, though not the final one.

Attention could also be drawn to the fact that in **74** 21 the stranger is mentioned for the first time in Part II.

Additionally, students could examine and discuss Sylvia's perception of the heron, contrasting it with the stranger's perspective.

If students have not yet read past this point, and if time allows, they could try to imagine a suitable conclusion to the story, giving as much detail as possible about the way this conclusion could be presented.

### II b Sylvia "cannot" speak (**74** 25–**75** 16)

The story has a two-fold climax. The first is Sylvia's sighting of the heron; the second is her refusal to give the heron's secret away (**75** 4–9). The dramatic importance of the two passages is emphasized by the use of the present tense.

*1. What are Sylvia's deep-felt reasons for refusing to reveal the heron's secret? What particular words convey the idea that she has found a friend in the heron whom she refuses to betray?*
– **75** 13–14 ("she remembers...")

*2. The last sentence in the second-last paragraph employs the verb "cannot" three times (once it is understood):*
– Sylvia cannot speak.
– She cannot tell the heron's secret.
– She cannot give the heron's life away.

*a) What is the strength behind such a simple verb?*
The auxiliary verb "can", negative "cannot", refers to extremes: there is no "perhaps" or "maybe". It is impossible for Sylvia to betray the bird.

*b) What is the force that compels Sylvia to keep silent?*
No clear answer is given, except the idea of a unity of spirit between Sylvia and the bird ("together" **75** 14). It is as if the loyalty she shows to the bird is reciprocal.

*c) How has Sylvia changed through this experience?*
At the beginning of the story she is shy (**66** 16) and cannot speak to the stranger because of her fear (**67**; **71** 11–13). However, once she has taken "the daring step across into the old pine-tree" (**72** 30–31) and thus discovers the heron's secret, she is "well satisfied" (**74** 18), having won a victory over her own fear. Significantly, her first thought is to speak to the stranger and await his reaction. The fact that even after this victory she "cannot" speak has nothing to do with fear, but rather with loyalty. Silence becomes the assertion of her own will.

### II c  Epilogue (**75** 17–end)

The epilogue is the final denouement. It carries the story past the immediate situation.

*Define "loyalty".*
Loyalty is behaviour in which you stay firm in your friendship or support for someone or something (e.g. some cause). Three levels of loyalty may be discerned:
- Sylvia's loyalty towards the hunter
- Sylvia's loyalty towards the heron
- Nature's loyalty towards Sylvia for having saved a part of it

Note that the narrative perspective (point of view) of the last paragraph is that of an omniscient narrator who stands outside Sylvia's world but knows it intimately.

In the epilogue the reader is left to speculate as to Sylvia's future.

## 2. For further discussion

*1. Sylvia's conflict involves a choice between the heron and the young man. Why does she choose the heron? Do you think she has made the right choice? Give reasons.*

*2. List as many reasons as you can why people all over the world kill birds and animals. In which cases can such killing be justified?*

# Glossary of Literary Terms

**antagonist** [-'---]: the character in a story or drama who is opposed to the hero/heroine (or protagonist)

**characterization:** 1. the means used by an author to develop a character (e.g. by physical description, by presentation of the character's thoughts, by showing how others react, etc.) 2. the actual image of a character which is developed in the course of a story

**climax:** the point in a story or play when a crisis is reached and a resolution can be expected; often called the "turning point"

**dénouement** [ˌdeˈnuːmɑːŋ]: The outcome of the plot; the part of a play or story in which conflicts are resolved and mysteries or secrets explained

**diction**: the choice and use of words in writing

**exposition**: the part of a narrative or drama, usually at the beginning, in which important background information about the characters and events is given

**foreshadowing**: hints or clues in a story or play that suggest what will happen later

**hyperbole** [haɪˈpɜːbəlɪ]: exaggeration; e.g. He kissed her a thousand times

**irony**: deliberately created discrepancy between words and their intended meanings. There are two main kinds in literature: 1. verbal irony—when a character or the author/narrator says one thing and means s.th. completely different 2. dramatic irony—when a character says or does s.th. without realizing its real significance, which is evident to the reader/audience

**narrator**: the person in whose words a story is told. It may be told in the author's own voice, or in an adopted voice. In either case, the narrator can remain outside the story (speaking in the third person) or be part of it (speaking in the first person)

**periphrasis** [pəˈrɪfrəsɪs]: using a complicated way of writing or saying s.th. that could be expressed in simple words; e.g. The defender of society apprehended the fugitive from the law, i.e. The policeman arrested the criminal

**plot**: the sequence of events or actions in a work of literature

**point of view**: the way the narrator presents the characters and events in a story a) as a first-person narrative, restricted to that speaker's point of view, or b) as a third-person narrative. The third-person narrative can take different forms: 1. omniscient (all-knowing) point of view, revealing the thoughts of all the characters; 2. point of view of one character only (limited); 3. objective point of view ("camera-eye"), recording only those details which are seen and heard by an invisible witness

**protagonist** [-ˈ---]: the main character in a work of literature on whom the action centers, the hero/heroine; opposite: antagonist

**stream of consciousness**: (also: interior monologue) a style of writing that attempts to imitate the natural flow of a character's thoughts, feelings, mental images, memories as the character experiences them; e.g. "My handkerchief. He threw it. I remember. Did I not take it up? His hand groped vainly in his pockets. No, I didn't. Better buy one." (James Joyce, in *Ulysses*)

**style**: choice and arrangement of words, sentence structure, use of figurative language, rhythm and tone that determine a writer's form of expression